S0-AZC-719

Cover Photograph: Bébé Bru
20" tall
All original
Mrs. Richard Wright

Above photograph: F. G. Bébé
28" tall
Mrs. Richard Wright

2nd Blue Book of Dolls & Values

by Jan Foulke

Photographs by Howard Foulke

Published By HOBBY HOUSE PRESS

Riverdale, Maryland 20840

The doll prices given within this book are intended as value guides rather than arbitrarily set prices. Each doll price recorded here is actually a compilation. The retail prices in this book are recorded as accurately as possible but in the case of errors, typographical, clerical or otherwise, the author and publisher assume no liability nor responsibility for any loss incurred by users of this book

Additional Copies Available @$8.95 From
HOBBY HOUSE PRESS
4701 Queensbury Road
Riverdale, Maryland 20840

Printed in the United States of America

ISBN 0-87588-120-3

About This Book

In preparing this 2nd BLUE BOOK OF DOLLS AND VALUES, I have adhered to the objectives of Thelma Bateman who originated the idea for the first BLUE BOOK.She wanted a book which would help collectors identify dolls and learn more about them: dolls which they already own, those that they might like to own among the large variety pictured, those that are offered to them for purchase, or those which they just might be curious about. Also, she wanted to list the actual retail prices of the dolls discussed. This book achieves both of those objectives.

Dolls are listed alphabetically in the text by the name of the individual doll, the maker, or the type of doll. An extensive index has been provided at the back of the book for the reader's convenience in locating a specific doll. Of course, it would be impossible to include every doll in a volume of this size, but we have tried to include those which were either available, desirable, interesting or popular. For each doll, we have provided historical information, a description of the doll, and in most cases, a photograph.

The historical information given for each doll would have been much more difficult to compile were it not for the original research already published by Dorothy, Elizabeth and Evelyn Coleman and Johana G. Anderton. For this, we are indebted to them.

Also we would like to thank the many collectors and dealers who have written encouragements or offered kind words and suggestions about our work on this book. We have met many lovely and wonderful people as a result. And especially we thank those who allowed us to come into their homes and photograph their dolls. We appreciate their willingness to share their treasures with other doll collectors and to put up with having their furniture moved around and their dolls carried back and forth from cabinet to makeshift photographic studio.

The data on the prices were gathered from January to June 1976 from antique shops, auctions, doll shops, antique shows, advertisements in collectors' periodicals, lists from doll dealers, and purchases reported by friends. For some the rarer dolls we had to dip back a little farther to late 1975. The information was sorted, indexed, catalogued, and finally computed into the range of prices shown in this book. Hence, the figures used here are not our own valuations and judgments--they are the results of our research as to the actual retail prices at which these dolls were either sold or offered for sale.

In setting down a price, we used a range to allow for the variables discussed later which necessarily affect the price of any doll. All prices given for antique dolls are for those in overall good to better condition, but showing normal wear, unless specifically noted in the description accompanying that particular doll. Bisque and china heads should not be cracked or broken. The especially outstanding doll in absolutely mint condition, never played with, in the original box, or with original tagged clothes, would command a price far higher than those quoted. Prices given for modern dolls were for those in overall good to better condition with original hair and clothes except as noted. Again a never-played-with doll in original box would bring a higher price than noted.

Certain dolls are becoming increasingly difficult to find and are seldom offered at a show or advertised since most dealers usually have a list of customers waiting for these desirable dolls. If we did not find a sufficient number of these dolls offered to be sure of giving a reliable range, we reported the information which we could find and marked those prices with an "*". In a very few instances we would find none of a certain doll offered, so we resorted to estimates from reliable established dealers and collectors. These, too, are noted individually with an "*".

Our column in THE DOLL READER, a periodical published by Hobby House Press, will try to note any marked changes in doll prices and will sometimes feature dolls which we could not include in this book either because they were not available or because we did not have sufficient space.

No price guide is the final word--it can't provide the absolute answer of what to pay. Use it only as an aid in purchasing a doll. The final decision must be yours, for only you are on the scene actually examining the specific doll in question. No book can take the place of actual field experience. Before you buy, do a lot of looking. Ask questions. You will find that most dealers are glad to talk about their dolls and pleased to share their information with you.

And so, with these last thoughts, we present to you this second BLUE BOOK OF DOLLS AND VALUES.

Jan Foulke
Summer 1976

Determining Doll Prices

Doll collecting is an exciting hobby, but deciding whether or not to buy a specific doll to add to your collection, can be difficult in the face of the many variable factors which affect the value of the doll. Some of these have already been outlined by Janet Johl and Dorothy Coleman, but they are important enough to bear restatement and amplification. Hopefully, you will find in this chapter some helpful suggestions about what to look for and what to consider in purchasing a doll.

I have found very few people who buy dolls strictly as an investment. Although many collectors rationalize their purchases by saying that they are making a good investment, they are still actually buying the doll because they like it--it has appeal to them for some reason: perhaps as an object of artistic beauty, perhaps because it evokes some kind of sentiment, perhaps it fills some need that they feel, or perhaps it speaks to something inside them. When my daughter and I go doll shopping, we look at them all, but we only stop to examine closely and consider buying those which have some appeal for us. Thus, we more often find ourselves buying first with our hearts and second with our heads. Anyway, it is this personal feeling toward the doll that makes it of value to you.

After you decide that you like a doll, find out what it is. Certainly, the marks on dolls are important in determining a price for with a little luck, they might tell what the doll is, who made it, where, and sometimes when. A 20" tall doll marked A.M. 390 even though she is in good condition and well dressed, is plentiful and should not cost as much as the harder-to-find S&H 1279 girl in the same size and condition. Likewise, if the doll is tagged "Margaret O'Brien," you know it's a rare one; a "Patsy" would be far more common. Of course, many dolls are unmarked but after you have seen quite a few dolls, you begin to notice their individual and special characteristics, so that then you can often determine what a doll <u>probably</u> is.

But even the mark doesn't tell all. Two dolls from exactly the same mold could carry vastly different prices (and look entirely different) because of the quality of the work done on the doll. To command top price, a bisque doll should have lovely bisque, decoration, eyes, and hair. As you examine many dolls, you will see that the quality varies from head to head, even with dolls made from the same mold by one firm. Choose the best of that type for which you are looking that you can find. The bisque should be smooth and silky, not grainy, rough, peppered (tiny black specks), or pimply. The tinting should be subdued and even, not harsh and splotchy, although the amount of color acceptable is often a matter of personal preference, some collectors liking very pale white bisque and others preferring a little more pink. Since doll heads are hand painted, one of good quality should show artistic skill in the portrayal of the expression on the face and in details, such as the mouth, eyebrows and eyelashes. On a doll with molded hair, deep molding, an unusual hair style, and brush marks to give the air a more realistic look, would be details which are desirable. If a doll has a wig, the hair should be appropriate, if not original--a lovely human hair wig or good quality mohair. The eyes should have a natural and lifelike appearance, whether they are glass or painted. If a doll doesn't meet these standards, it should be priced lower than one that does.

Another factor which is important when pricing a doll is the condition. A doll with a crack on the face or extensive professional repair would sell for considerably less than a doll with only normal wear; a hairline or a small professional repair in an inconspicuous place would decrease the value somewhat, but not nearly so much. Sometimes a head will have a factory flaw which occurred in the making, such as a cooking crack, scratch, piece of kiln debris, or a ridge not smoothed out. The factory was producing toys for a profit, not works of art, so they did not discard all heads with slight flaws, especially if they were in an inconspicuous place or could be covered. If these factory defects are slight and not detracting, they have little or no effect on the value of the doll, and whether or not to purchase such a doll would be a matter of personal opinion. You almost have to expect an old doll to show minor wear; perhaps there's a rub on the nose (a vulnerable spot), wear on the hair of an old papier-mâché or china head doll, or scuffed toes or missing fingers on an old composition body--these are to be expected and do not affect the value of the doll. Certainly, an old doll in never-played-with condition, all original hair and clothes, labeled, in its original box is every collector's dream--and would carry the highest of all prices for that type. Unless the doll is rare and you particularly want it, do not pay top price for a doll which needs extensive work: restringing, setting eyes, replacing body parts, new wig, dressing--all these repairs add up to a considerable sum at the doll hospital. As for the composition dolls, you should expect a more nearly perfect condition if you are paying top price--original hair, clothes, little or no crazing, good coloring, tag, if possible. However, dolls in this condition are becoming harder to find. Pay less for a doll which doesn't have original clothes; even less for a damaged one. On the hard plastics and vinyls, you should expect mint condition for top price; original clothes would be a must.

Check over the body of the doll. For a top price, an old doll should have the original or an appropriate old body in good condition. If a doll does not have the right body, you could conceivably end up with not a complete doll, but with two parts--head and body--not worth as much as one whole doll. Minor damage or repair to an old body scarcely affects the value of the doll. An original body carefully repaired is preferable to a new one. If you have a choice, a good quality ball-jointed composition body is more desirable than a crudely made five-piece body or a stick type body with just pieces of wood for upper arms and legs, but unfortunately many of the small German character heads came on these crude bodies, and collectors just have to live with them. Occasionally the body adds value to the head. For instance, a small six-inch doll with a completely jointed body, or a French fashion with jointed wood body, or a doll with a lady-type body, or a doll with a jointed-toddler-type body would all be more desirable because of their bodies. On the all-composition dolls a body in poor condition, cracked and peeling, greatly reduces the value of the doll.

Look at the clothing critically in considering the value of the doll. It should be appropriate for the doll, made in types of fabrics and styles which would have been in vogue when the doll was produced. Original clothes are, of course, highly desirable and even carefully mended ones would be preferable to new clothes. However, it is often difficult to determine whether or not the clothes are original or simply just old. Many old dolls came undressed or clad only in a chemise and were dressed at home. A doll with original clothes is certainly more valuable, but whether or not these clothes are retained on the doll seems to be a matter of personal preference among collectors, many of whom enjoy dressing their own dolls. If you do feel that you want to redress your dolls, show respect for the original clothes and keep them in a labeled bag or box for giving to the next owner should you ever sell your doll, or pass it down to a younger member of the family, for dolls are heirlooms and you are only the keeper for a short time in history.

Having already discussed body, wig, eyes, and clothes, this would seem to be a good place to put in a word about the total originality of a doll. Some collectors feel that a doll which they are sure has all original parts and clothes is more valuable than one which has replaced wig, body parts, eyes, pate, clothes, etc. They try to be sure that the head and body and all other parts are not only appropriate, but have always been together. Of course, this is not always possible to determine when a doll has seen hard play for several generations or has passed through many hands before reaching the collector. But sometimes if you know the original source of the doll, you can be reasonably sure by using a little knowledge as well as common sense. Again this is a matter of personal preference and totally original dolls nowadays are few and far between.

Take into account the size of the doll in determining the price. Usually price and size are related for a certain type of doll--a smaller size is lower, a larger size is higher. The greatest variances of price to size occur at the extremes, either a very small or a very large doll. On the large side, bisque head dolls, especially over 30" are in demand and rising in price; the large 36" vinyl Shirley Temple and the 30" composition Patsy Mae are practically unavailable. On the tiny side, the small closed-mouth Jumeau and Wee Patsy are examples in the opposite direction, bringing higher prices than comparable average-sized dolls.

A final point to consider in pricing your doll is the age of the doll. An early Queen Anne wood doll would be more greatly valued than a late 19th Century penny wooden. However, curiously enough to some, the oldest dolls do not necessarily command the highest prices. A lovely old china head with exquisite work and very unusual hairdo would bring a good price, but not as much as a 20th Century S.F.B.J. 252 Pouty. Many desirable composition dolls of 1930's are selling at prices higher than older bisque dolls of 1900-1920. So, in determining price the age of the doll, may or may not be significant, according to the specific type.

So far, except for the aspect of personal appeal, the factors which we have considered in pricing a doll have been physical and tangible--the marks, the quality of craftsmanship, condition, clothing, size, and age. But there are still several others; these might be called the intangible factors.

Perhaps most important here would be the availability of the doll--how easy or difficult it is to find. Each year brings more new doll collectors than it brings newly-discovered desirable old dolls; hence, the supply is diminished. As long as the demand for certain antique and collectible dolls is greater than the supply, prices will rise. This explains the gigantic increase in the prices of less common dolls, such as the Brus, K(star)R and S.F.B.J. characters, and googlies which were made for only a limited period of time, and the more gentle rise in dolls which are fairly common, primarily, the German girl or child dolls which were made over a longer period of time. The price you pay should be consistent with the availability of the doll.

Sometimes, however, it is the popularity of a certain doll which makes the price rise. This is currently true with dolls such as Shirley Temple and the Bye-lo baby which still seem to be fairly plentiful, yet rising in price, because they are popular and many collectors want them enough to be willing to pay a price that might be higher than the availability factor warrants.

Sometimes the uniqueness of a doll makes price determination very difficult. If you never have seen a doll exactly like it before, and it isn't given in the price guide or pictured in any books, deciding what to pay can be a problem, especially if you are not sure of the reliability of the seller. In this case, you have to use the knowledge you have as a frame of reference in which to place the doll. For instance, you find a doll which you really like, 18" tall girl marked A.M. 2000. It isn't pictured anywhere and you can't find it in the price guide--yet you've looked at hundreds of dolls and have never seen one before, so you know from experience it's not common. The dealer is asking $35 more than the price of a common number A.M. girl. You have to decide on your own whether or not the doll is worth the price to you. (I think it would be!)

Of course, another important factor which helps determine what price goes on the doll in the shop, is the price the dealer had to pay for it. In buying a doll, a dealer has to consider everything discussed here, in addition to whether or not there is the possibility of making a reasonable profit on the doll. Contrary to what many collectors believe, dealers in antique dolls do not make enormous profits. Their margin of profit is not nearly so high as that of the proprietor of a shop which sells new items. This is primarily due to the availability factor already discussed. Old dolls cannot be ordered from a wholesale catalogue. Fewer are turning up in attics. Most are coming from collections, whose owners, understandably enough, want to get as much as they can for their dolls. To the price which he must pay a dealer adds his percentage of profit and comes up with a dollar amount for the tag.

The last factor to consider about doll prices is that the price guide gives the retail price of a doll if obtained from a dealer, whereas actually a doll might have several types of buying prices. This idea is pointed out by Ceil Chandler. First, a dealer when buying stock could not pay the prices listed; he must buy somewhat lower if he expects to sell at a profit. In order to obtain stock, a dealer looks to private individuals who may have dolls in an attic (and there are fewer and fewer of these with truly desirable dolls), auctions, collectors, and other dealers as possible sources--all of which are also available to collectors who can purchase from these sources at the same prices that dealers can. Second, a dealer would expect to pay less per doll if he bought a collection or a large lot than if he purchased them individually. A third type of price would prevail if a collector buys from another collector; in this case, you would probably pay less than when buying from a dealer. The fourth type of price is the "lucky" price you might find at a shop, garage sale, flea market, or just about anywhere that there might be an old doll.

Hopefully, in this chapter, we have presented some ideas which might be of help to you in purchasing your next doll or in evaluating dolls which you already own. And we hope that you will enjoy many, many hours of pleasure as you build your doll collection.

Jan Foulke
August 1974
Revised, June 1976

A.M. Character Baby

MAKER: Armand Marseille of Köppelsdorf, Thüringia, Germany

DATE: 1910 - on

MATERIAL: Bisque head, bent-limb composition body

SIZE: Various

MARK: "A.M." and/or "ARMAND MARSEILLE" plus "Germany" and numbers such as 990, 992, 985, 971, etc.

Armand Marseille
Germany
990
A 9/0 M

Marked A.M. Baby: Bisque head, composition bent-limb body, sleep eyes, open mouth - some with teeth, good wig, suitably dressed; all in nice condition. Mold #990, 985, 971 and other common numbers:

Size	
8-9"	$100-125
11-14"	$150-185
16-18"	$200-225
21-24"	$275-315

A.M. 990
17" tall
(H&J Foulke)

A.M. Character Children

MAKER: Armand Marseille of Köppelsdorf, Thüringia, Germany
DATE: 1910 - on
MATERIAL: Bisque socket head, composition body; sometimes shoulder head on kid body
SIZE: Various
MARK: A.M. Germany and numbers such as 500, 550, 600, 590, etc.

Germany
550
A 3 M
DRGM

A.M. Character Child: Bisque head, glass or painted eyes, molded hair or wig, open or closed mouth. Composition body. Dressed. All in good condition.

Mold #500 8 - 10" $200-275; Mold #560a 11-15" $200-250
Mold #590 15 - 16" $550-650; Mold #600 12-14" $300-325

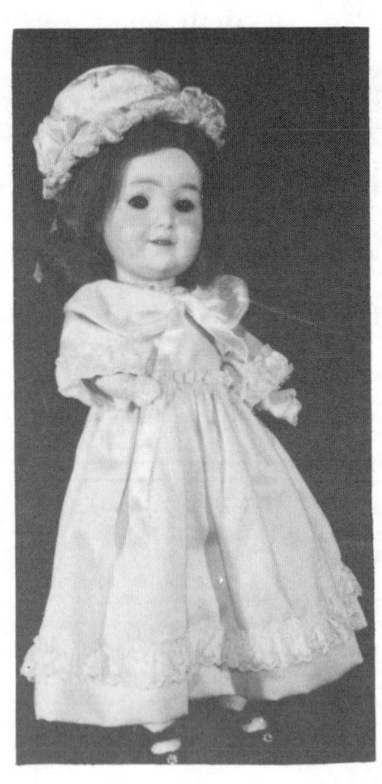

Left: A.M. 560a/Germany 11" tall (H. & J. Foulke)
Right: A.M. 590/Germany 17" tall (Richard Wright)

A.M. Child Doll

MAKER: Armand Marseille of Köppelsdorf, Thüringia, Germany
DATE: Ca. 1890 - on
MATERIAL: Bisque head, composition ball-jointed body; bisque shoulder head, jointed kid body with bisque lower arms
SIZE: Various
MARK: "A. M." and/or "ARMAND MARSEILLE" plus numbers, such as 390, 1894, 370, 3200, and/or "Germany". Also sometimes horseshoe mark.

Armand Marseille
Germany.
370
A 6 M

Marked A. M. Child Doll: Bisque head, composition ball-jointed body, nice wig, set or sleep eyes, open mouth, pretty clothes; all in good condition.

Mold #390, 370		Size 28-29"	$200-250
Size 8-9"	$75-85	Size 36"	$450-500
Size 14-16"	$100-125	Size 39-44	$700-900
Size 22-25"	$150-175	*Mold #1894 slightly higher	

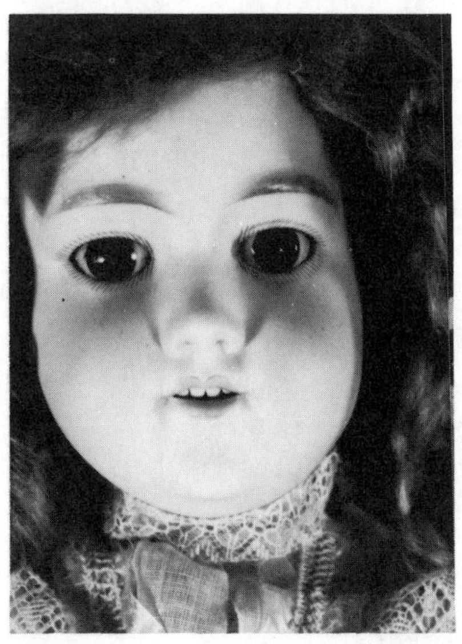

Left: A. M. 390, 24" tall, all original (H & J Foulke)
Right: A. M. 1894, 23" tall, all original except hat (H & J Foulke)

A.M. Infant

MAKER: Armand Marseille of Köppelsdorf, Thüringia, Germany
DATE: 1924 - on
MATERIAL: Bisque head, cloth or sometimes composition body
SIZE: Various
MARK: A.M. 351 (open mouth) or 341 (closed mouth)

Marked A.M. Infant: Solid dome bisque head with molded and/or painted hair, sleep eyes, cloth or composition body, all in good condition. Dressed.

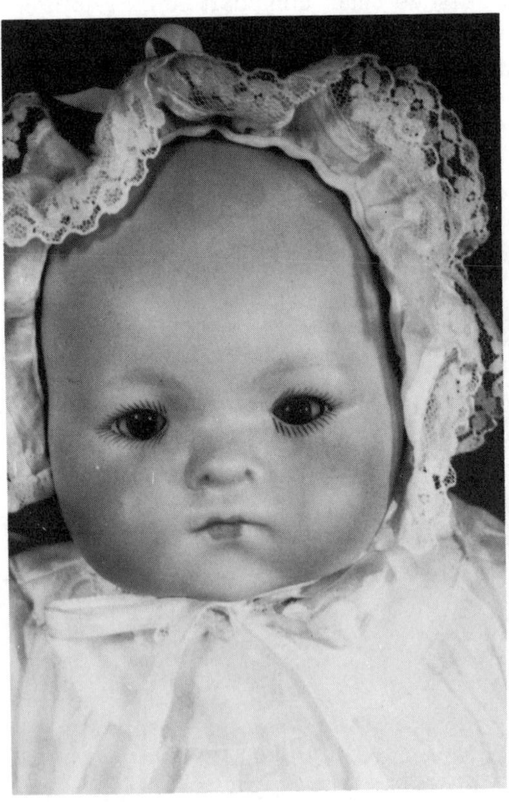

#351, open mouth
10-12" $125-165
16-20" $200-250

#341, closed mouth
10-12" $125-165
14-16" $200-250

"A.M. 341
Made in Germany"
16" long
(H&J Foulke)

A.M. Lady

MAKER: Armand Marseille of Köppelsdorf, Thüringia, Germany
DATE: 1910 - 1930
MATERIAL: Bisque head, composition body
SIZE: Usually 10" - 15"
MARK:

Armand Marseille
Germany
401
A 5/0 M

A.M. Lady: Bisque head with mature face, mohair wig, sleeping eyes, closed mouth; composition lady body with molded bust, long slender arms and legs; appropriate clothes; all in good condition. $400*

Painted bisque $250*

*Not enough price samples to justify a reliable range.

A.M. 401
12-1/2" tall
(Mike White)

A.T.

MAKER: Probably by A. Thuillier, Paris, France
DATE: 1875-1890
MATERIAL: Bisque socket head on wooden, kid, or composition body
SIZE: Size 2 is usually 12"; size 14 is 29"
MARK: A.T. and size number (2 - 14 known)

AT·N° 8

Marked A.T.: Perfect bisque head, paperweight eyes, pierced ears, closed mouth, cork pate, good wig. Body of wood, kid or composition in good condition. Appropriate clothes.

Size 20" $6,000

For photo see COLLECTOR'S ENCYCLOPEDIA OF DOLLS by the Colemans, page 616, #1623 A, B and C.

A.W. Bisque

MAKER: Adolf Wislizenus of Waltershausen, Thüringia, Germany
DATE: About 1890 - on
MATERIAL: Bisque head, composition ball-jointed body
SIZE: Various
MARK: "A.W.", "A.W." over "W", "A.W. SPECIAL", sometimes with "Germany" added, sometimes "OLD GLORY" etc.

Wislizenus Doll: Marked bisque head, composition ball-jointed body, blue or brown sleep eyes, open mouth, good wig, dressed. All in good condition. Size 24-26" $145-175

Marked "A.W. Special 2" 22 inch Doll in Arms-- Mme. Alexander "Wendy" 8 inch.

Photo by Thelma Bateman

ABG Character Doll

MAKER: Alt, Beck & Gottschalck, Nauendorf, Thuringia, Germany
DATE: Ca. 1910 on
MATERIAL: Bisque head, composition body
SIZE: Various
MARK: "Made in Germany"
(Numbers, such as 1361 found underneath mark)

Marked ABG Character: Bisque head, open mouth, sleep eyes, good wig, open nostrils; composition body; suitably dressed; nice condition.with bent-limb baby body.

Size 12-14" $140-165*
Size 18-20" $250-275*

*Allow extra for toddler body.

"ABG 1352/38"
Flirty-eyes
16" tall
(H&J Foulke)

ABG Child Doll

MAKER: Alt, Beck & Gottschalck, Nauendorf, Thuringia, Germany
DATE: Ca. 1893 on
MATERIAL: Bisque heads, composition ball-jointed bodies
SIZE: Various
MARK: "Made in Germany"
(Numbers, such as 1362, underneath mark)

Marked Child Doll: Bisque head, good wig, sleep eyes, open mouth; ball-jointed body; dressed, all in good condition.

17-20" $125-150
32-35" $300-400

"ABG
1362
Made in Germany"
24" tall
(Joyce Alderson)

Alexander Girl

MAKER: Alexander Doll Co., New York, N.Y., U.S.A.
DATE: 1930's
MATERIAL: All composition
SIZE: 7 inches
MARK: "Mme. Alexander" on back; various labels to identify specific doll

---

Alexander Girl: All composition with one piece head and body, jointed shoulders and hips, mohair wig, painted eyes. Original clothes. All in good condition. Size 7" $30-35

"Finnish
Mme. Alexander"
7" tall
All Original
(H&J Foulke)

Alice in Wonderland

MAKER: Alexander Doll Co., New York, N.Y., U.S.A.
DATE: Ca. 1923
MATERIAL: All cloth
SIZE: 16 inches
MARK: Dress tagged "Original/Alice in Wonderland/Trade-Mark 304, 488/Madame Alexander"

Cloth Alice: Cloth body with one-piece arms and legs sewed on. Molded mask face, yellow yarn hair, painted blue eyes. Original dress. All in good condition.

16" $175-225*
* Not enough price samples to justify a reliable range.

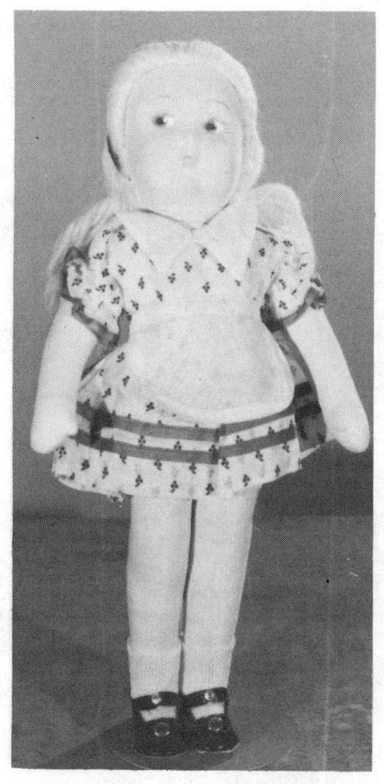

"Alice in Wonderland"
16"
All original
(Ann Tardie)

All-Bisque Baby

MAKER: Various German firms
DATE: Ca. 1900 - on
MATERIAL: Bisque
SIZE: Various
MARK: Some with "Germany" and/or numbers

All-bisque Baby: Jointed at shoulders and hips, curved arms and legs, molded and painted hair, painted eyes, very good workmanship; not dressed; all in good condition.
Size 2-1/2 to 3-1/2" $30-40
Size 5-6" $55-75

Pink bisque, not finely painted (Candy Babies) Size 3" $30-40

Same as the first All-bisque Baby, but with character face.
Size 4-5" $95-125

Same as the first All-bisque Baby, but with glass eyes and swivel neck Size 4-5" $225-250

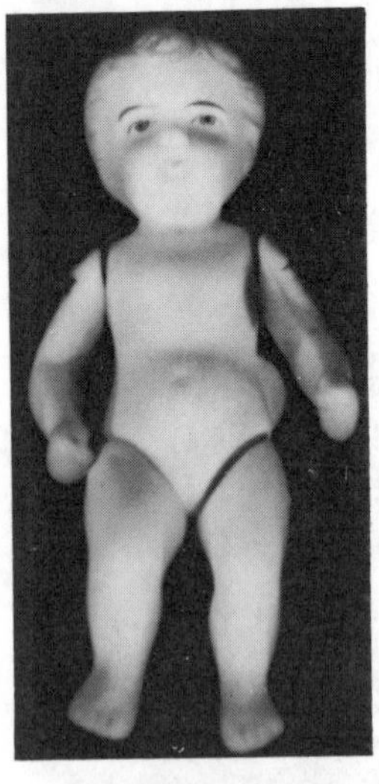

All-bisque baby
Unmarked
3-1/2" long
(H&J Foulke)

All-bisque
"Candy" Baby
2-1/2" long
All original
(H&J Foulke)

All-Bisque Characters

(German)

MAKER: Various German firms
DATE: 1913 - on
MATERIAL: All bisque
SIZE: Various small sizes
MARK: Various

A. Hoofed "The Little Imp" 7" $150-175*
B. The Medic $65
C. Cupid or Sister 5-1/2" $40-50
D. Baby Bud 4-5" $125*
E. Wide-Awake Doll 9" $125*
F. Our Fairy 9" $700*
G. Boy with sword and removable hat 6-7" $75*
H. Peterkin 10-1/2" $250-300*
I. Orsini DiDi or MiMi 5-1/2" $600*

*Not enough price samples to justify a reliable range.

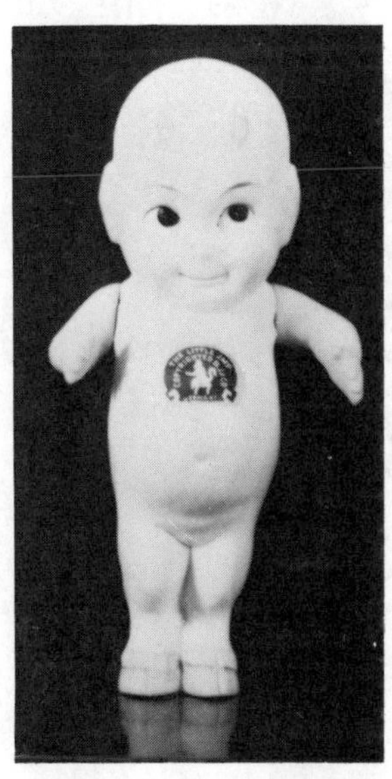

Left: "The Little Imp"; 7" tall (Richard Wright)
Right: "The Medic"; 4" tall (H&J Foulke)

All-Bisque Child Doll

(Glass eyes, French type)

MAKER: Various French and German firms
DATE: Ca. 1880 - on
MATERIAL: Bisque
SIZE: Various
MARK: None

All-Bisque French Doll: Jointed at shoulders and hips, slender arms and legs, glass eyes, good wig, closed mouth, molded shoes or boots and stockings, dressed or undressed; all in good condition.

Stationary neck:		Swivel neck:	
Size 3-4"	$65-85	Size 5"	$250-300
Size 6"	$150-175	Size 6"	$350-400
		Size 8-1/2"	$475-525

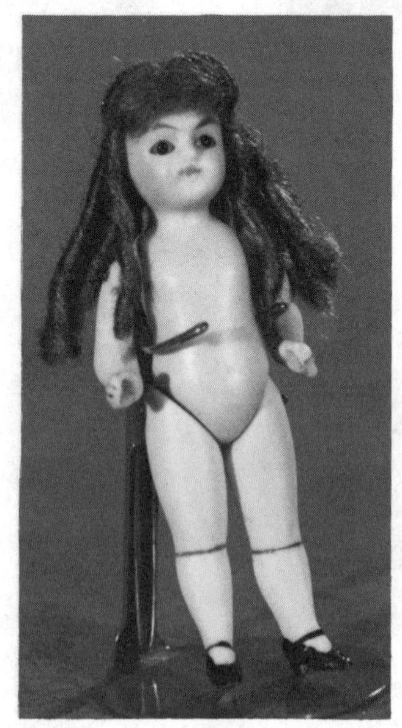

French-type
4" tall
Stationary neck
(Beth Foulke)

All-Bisque Child Doll

(Glass eyes, German)

MAKER: Various German firms
DATE: Ca. 1880 - on
MATERIAL: Bisque
SIZE: Various
MARK: Some with "Germany" and/or numbers

All-Bisque German Doll: Jointed at shoulders and hips, glass eyes, good wig, closed or open mouth, molded and painted shoes and stockings; dressed or undressed; all in good condition.

Stationary neck, good quality, Size 4-5" $90-120, 7 to 7-1/2" $140-180, 8 to 8-1/2" $225

Swivel neck, Size 4 to 5-1/2" $150-200

Later, not as good quality, stationary neck, Size 4-5" $75
Size 7" $100-125

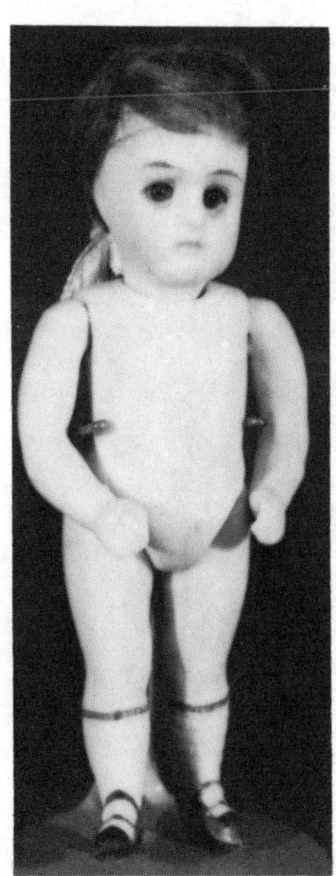

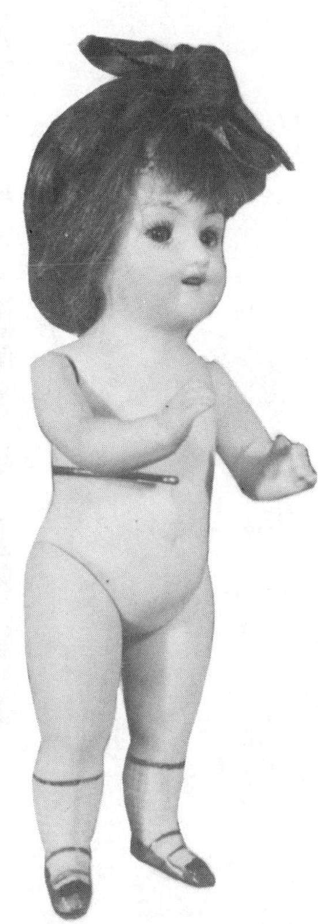

Left: "620" All bisque, swivel neck, 4" tall (H&J Foulke)

Right: "150", 7" tall (H&J Foulke)

All-Bisque Child Doll
(Molded Clothes)

MAKER: Various German firms
DATE: Ca. 1880 - on
MATERIAL: Bisque
SIZE: Various
MARK: Usually only numbers

All-Bisque with molded clothes: Jointed only at shoulders, molded and painted clothes or underwear; molded and painted hair, sometimes with molded hat; painted eyes, closed mouth, molded shoes and socks (if in underwear often barefoot); good quality work; all in good condition.

Size 4" $55-65
Size 5" $75-85
Size 6-7" $100-150

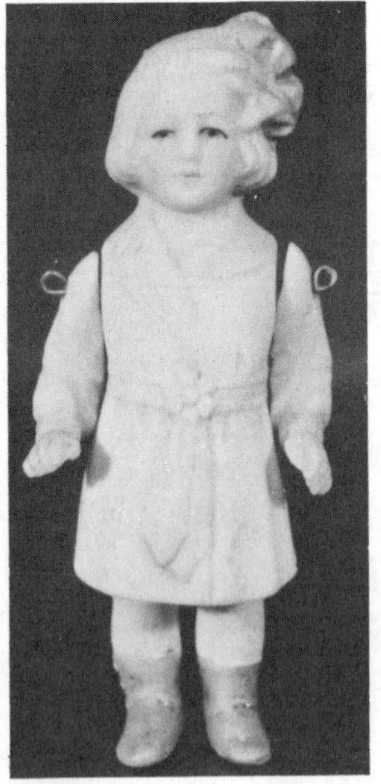

All-bisque girl
with molded clothes
3-3/4" tall
(H&J Foulke)

All-Bisque Child Dolls

(Nippon)

MAKER: Various Japanese firms
DATE: Ca. 1915 - on
MATERIAL: Bisque
SIZE: Various small sizes
MARK: "NIPPON"

All-Bisque Child Doll Marked "Nippon": Jointed at shoulders only, molded and painted hair and eyes, may have ribbed socks and one-strap shoes; some with molded clothes; some not dressed; all in good condition.

4-5" $20-30
6-7" $30-35
"Baby Darling" 4-1/2 - 5-1/2" $25-35
"Queue San Baby" 3-1/2 - 4-1/2" $50-65

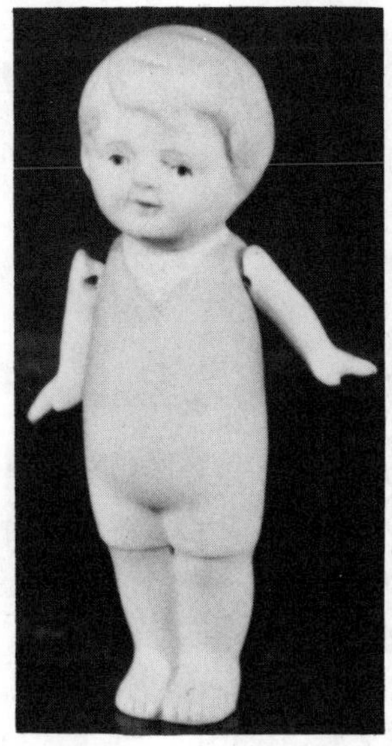

Nippon Doll
4-3/4" tall
(H&J Foulke)

All-Bisque Child Doll

(Painted Eyes)

MAKER: Various German firms
DATE: Ca. 1880 on
MATERIAL: Bisque
SIZE: Various
MARK: Some with "Germany" and/or numbers

All-bisque German Doll: Jointed at shoulders and hips, stationary neck, painted eyes, molded and painted hair or mohair wig, molded and painted shoes and stockings, closed mouth, fine quality work, dressed or undressed; all in good condition.

	Size 4-5"	$65-85
Molded hair, later, not as good quality.	Size 4-5"	$35-45
Later pink bisque with wig.	Size 3-1/2 to 4-1/2"	$35-40

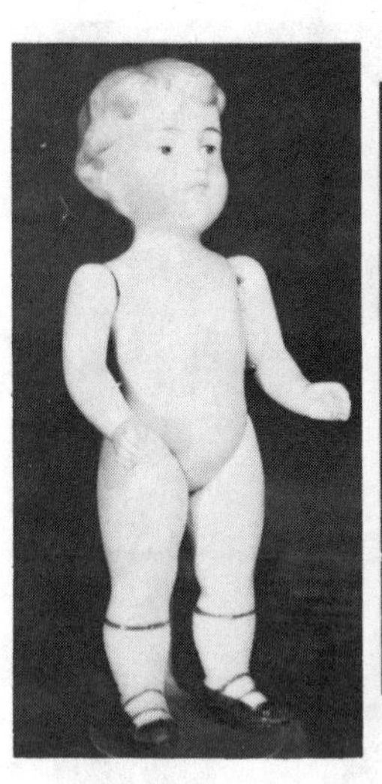

Left: "160-4"; 5-1/2" tall; fine quality (H&J Foulke)
Middle: "8929/I"; 4-3/4" tall; later, not so fine quality (H&J Foulke)
Right: 3-1/2"; pink bisque (H&J Foulke)

All-Bisque Dolls

(Made in Japan)

MAKER: Various Japanese firms
DATE: Ca. 1915 - on
MATERIAL: Bisque
SIZE: Various small sizes
MARK: "Made in Japan"

Baby doll with bent limbs, jointed shoulders and hips, molded and painted hair and eyes; not dressed; all in good condition.
White Bisque 4" $15-20 Black Bisque 4" $15

Child doll with jointed shoulders, legs together, sometimes with molded clothes. 4-6" $15-20

Stiff characters with molded and painted clothes 3-4" $3-6

Disney Characters marked "© Walt E. Disney" with name of character. 3-4" $7.50 up
Mickey or Minnie 4-5" $25-35

Betty Boop-type 6-7" $12-15

All-bisque Oriental
"Made in Japan"
3" tall
(H&J Foulke)

All-Bisque Flappers

MAKER: Various German firms
DATE: 1920
MATERIAL: All bisque
SIZE: 3 inches
MARK: "Germany"

Flappers: Pink bisque with wire joints at shoulders and hips; molded bobbed hair and painted features, painted shoes and socks, original factory clothes; all in good condition.

Size 3" $30-35

Flappers
3"
All original
(H & J Foulke)

All-Bisque Nodders

MAKER: Various German and Japanese firms
DATE: Ca. 1920
MATERIAL: Bisque
SIZE: Up to 4-1/4"
MARK: Germany or Nippon

All-Bisque Characters: Nodding heads (elastic strung), molded clothes; all in good condition.

German: 3" $25-30
Comic Characters: 4" $40-45
Nippon: 3-3-1/2" $20-25

"Nippon"/Nodder; 3-1/2" tall (H&J Foulke)

American Children

MAKER: EFFanBEE Doll Do., New York, N.Y., U.S.A.
DATE: 1936 - 1939
MATERIAL: All composition
SIZE: 15", 18", 21"
DESIGNER: Dewees Cochran
MARK: "EFFanBEE/American/Children" (head)
"EFFanBEE/Anne Shirley"(body)

EFF AN BEE
ANNE SHIRLEY

American Children: Composition swivel head on composition body jointed at shoulders and hips. Four different faces all with sleep eyes, closed mouths, and human hair wigs. Original clothes. All in good condition.

Size 15-21" $125-150

For photo see TWENTIETH CENTURY DOLLS by Anderton, page 196, illustration F & B 42.

American School Boy

MAKER: Unknown German firms
DATE: Ca. 1870's into 1890's
MATERIAL: Bisque shoulder head, kid or cloth (or combination) body
SIZE: Various
MARK: Some with numbers and/or "Germany"

Molded Hair Child: Bisque shoulder head, molded blond hair (sometimes brown hair), glass eyes, kid or cloth body, good bisque or kid arms, closed mouth, nicely dressed; all in good condition. Size 12-16" $300-450

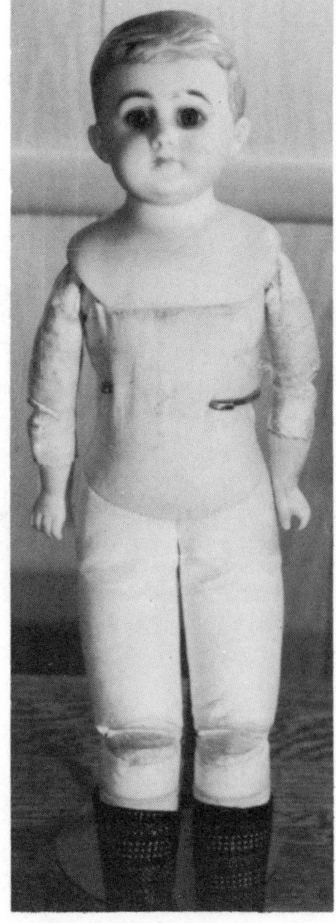

So-called
American School Boy
17" tall
(Bertha Neumyer)

Amosandra

MAKER: Barr Rubber Products Co., Sandusky, Ohio, U.S.A.
DATE: 1949
MATERIAL: Rubber
SIZE: Various
DESIGNER: Ruth E. Newton
MARK: "Columbia Broadcasting System, Inc. Designed by Ruth E. Newton"

Amosandra Marked Rubber Baby: Adorable jointed bent-limb baby doll, original clothes; all in good condition.

Size 9-12" $18-25

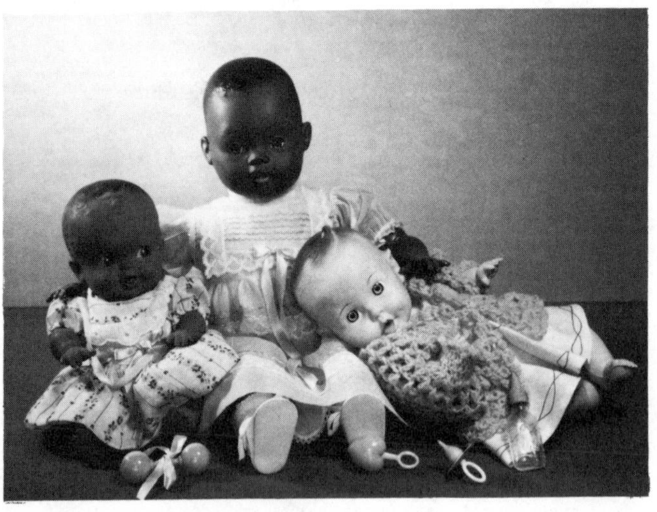

Left: "Amosandra © Columbia Broadcasting System, Inc. Designed by Ruth E. Newton" 7" seated

Middle: Ideal's "Saralee"

Right: Sun Rubber's "Gerber Baby"

Photo by Thelma Bateman

Art Fabric Mills

MAKER: Art Fabric Mills, New York City, N.Y., U.S.A. (1899-1910); Selchow & Righter were sole distributors and in 1911 they were the successors (1911-1923)
DATE: 1899 - 1923
MATERIAL: Printed on cloth to be cut out, sewed and stuffed
SIZE: 6-1/2" to 30"
MARK: On foot as pictured below.

Marked Art Fabric Mills Doll: Features and underclothes printed on cloth. Good condition (some soil acceptable). Undressed.

Size 6"	$15-18
Size 18"	$30-35
Size 25"	$60-70

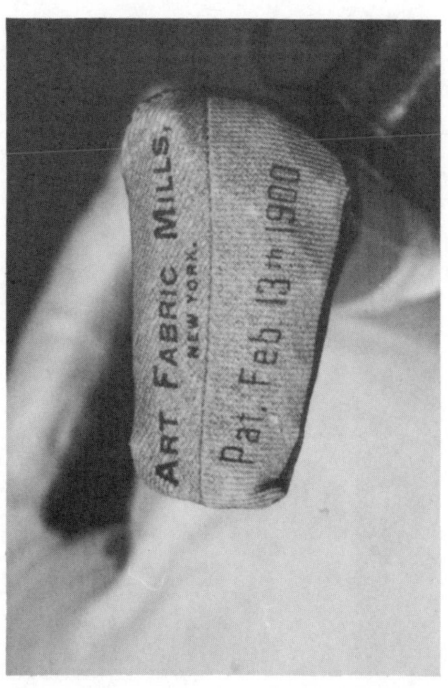

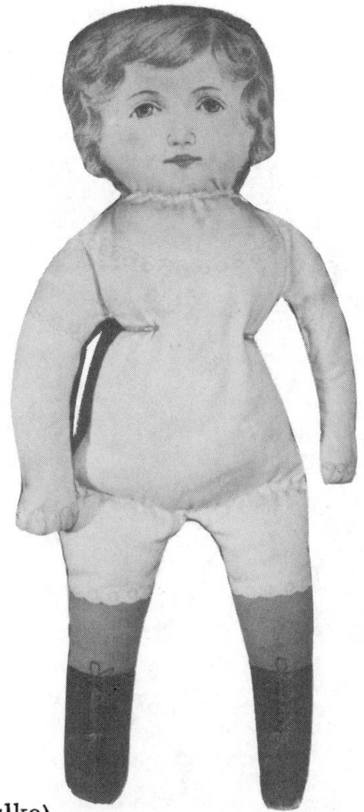

Art Fabric Mills, 18" tall, (Jan Foulke)

Autoperipatetikos

(Walking Doll)

MAKERS: David S. Cohen & Joseph Lyon & Co. of New York, N.Y.; Martin & Runyon of London, England and others.

DATE: 1862 - Patented by Enoch Rice Morrison, N.Y., N.Y.

MATERIAL: Heads made of pale bisque, china, cloth or papier-mâché. Under the skirt is the mechanism enclosed in a cardboard bell. The base of this bell is a circle of wood with slits where the metal feet protrude.

SIZE: 10 inches

MARK: "Patented, July 15, 1862" found on underside of wooden circle.

Patented July 15th, 1862; also, in England.

Marked Autoperipatetikos: Head of china, bisque, cloth or papier-mâché, leather arms, original clothes or nicely dressed. In working order. Size 10" $650 up*

*Not enough price samples to justify a reliable range.

Autoperipatetikos
China head
10" tall
(Bertha Neumyer)

Baby Bo Kaye

MAKER: Heads - Cameo Doll Co. (composition)
J.D. Kestner (bisque)
Bodies - K & K Toy Co.
DATE: 1925
MATERIAL: Bisque or composition flange neck, head; composition limbs, cloth body.
SIZE: About 18"
DESIGNER: J.L. Kallus
MARK: "J.L. Kallus: Copr. Germany
1394/30"

Baby Bo Kaye: Bisque head marked as above, molded hair, glass eyes, open mouth with two lower teeth. Body as above. Dressed. All in good condition.

Bisque $1,200 (very rare)*
Celluloid $150-200

*Not enough price samples to justify a reliable range.

Baby BoKaye
Celluloid Head
16" tall
(Clendenien Collection)

Baby Dainty
(EFFanBEE)

MAKER: EFFanBEE Doll Corp., New York, N.Y., U.S.A. (Bernard Fleischaker and Hugo Baum)

DATE: Ca. 1912 - 1922

MATERIAL: Composition shoulder head, cloth body, composition arms and legs; jointed at shoulders and hips.

SIZE: Usually 13-15"

MARK: "EFFANBEE
BABY DAINTY"

EFFANBEE
BABY DAINTY

Marked Baby Dainty: Composition shoulder head, painted molded hair, painted facial features (sometimes with tin sleep eyes), cloth stuffed body jointed at shoulders and hips, with curved arms and straight legs of composition. Original or appropriate old clothes; all in good condition.

Size 15" $35-45

"Effanbee
Baby Dainty"
15" tall
Original dress
(H&J Foulke)

Baby Dimples
(Horsman)

MAKER: E.I. Horsman Co.
DATE: 1928 - 1932 (at least)
MATERIAL: Composition head, arms and legs; cloth torso
SIZE: 14" - 22"
MARK: On head

©
E.I.H. CO. INC.

Baby Dimples: Composition head with smiling face, open mouth, tin sleep eyes, molded and painted hair; soft cloth body with composition arms and legs. Original or appropriate old clothes. All in good condition.

Size 17-22" $45-55

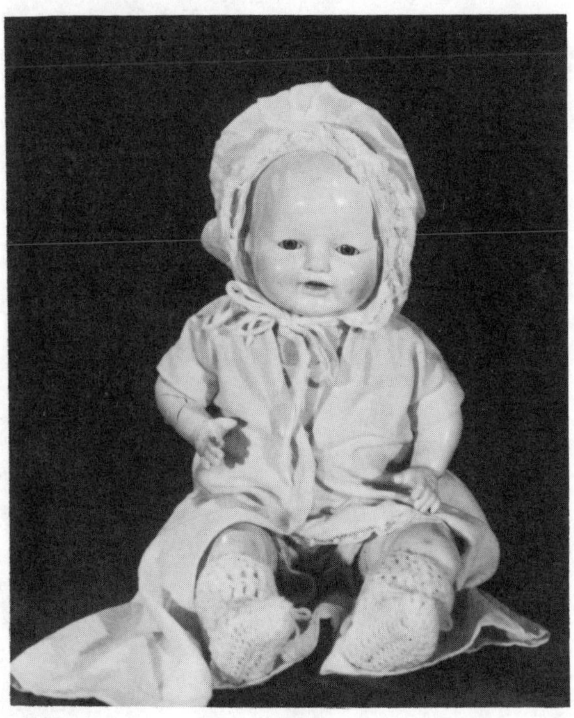

Baby Dimples, 17" tall
(Emily Manning)

Baby Grumpy
(EFFanBEE)

MAKER: Fleischaker & Baum, New York, N.Y., U.S.A.
DATE: 1912 - 1939
MATERIAL: Molded composition shoulder head and limbs, cloth body, white and black
SIZE: 11-1/2" and larger
MARK: Effanbee

EFFANBEE
BABY GRUMPY
COPYR. 1923

Marked "Baby Grumpy": Composition shoulder head with frowning face, molded and painted hair, painted eyes, closed mouth, composition arms and legs, cloth body, dressed; all in good condition.

Size 12" $60-70

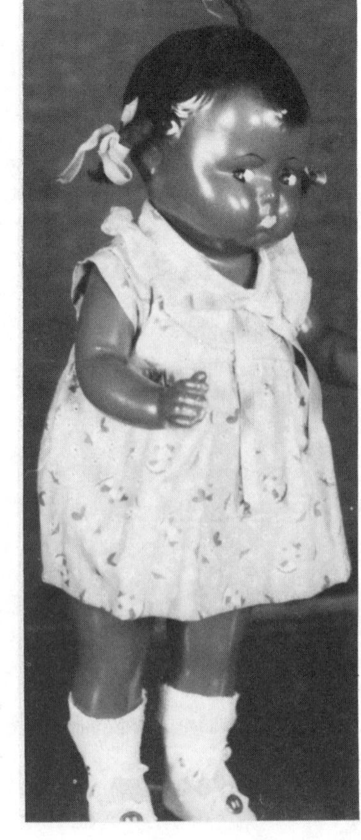

Black
Baby Grumpy
12" tall
All original
(H&J Foulke)

Baby Jane

MAKER: Alexander Doll Co., New York, N.Y., U.S.A.
DATE: Ca. 1930's
MATERIAL: All composition
SIZE: 16 inches
MARK: Baby Jane/ Reg Mme. Alexander (on head)

Marked Baby Jane: All composition with swivel head, jointed hips and shoulders, sleeping eyes, open mouth, mohair wig. Original clothes. All in good condition.

Size 16" $100-125*

*Not enough price samples to justify a reliable range.

For photo see MORE TWENTIETH CENTURY DOLLS, page 518, illustration ALEX-79.

Baby Peggy (Montgomery)

MAKER: L. Amberg & Son, New York and Germany
DATE: 1924
MATERIAL: Bisque head, composition or kid jointed body
SIZE: 18-21" tall
MARK: "19 © 24/LA&S/NY GERMANY"

Baby Peggy: Bisque head with smiling face, closed mouth, brown sleeping eyes, brown bobbed mohair wig; jointed body. Dressed or undressed. All in good condition. Size 18-21" $850

For illustration see American Collectors Dolls, page 109

Baby Phyllis

MAKER: Baby Phyllis Doll Co., Brooklyn, N.Y., U.S.A. Heads by Armand Marseille
DATE: 1925 on
MATERIAL: Bisque head on cloth body
SIZE: Various
MARK: BABY PHYLLIS
Made in Germany
24014

Marked Baby Phyllis: Perfect bisque solid-dome head, glass eyes, closed mouth, cloth body. Appropriate clothes.

10 - 12" $300-350*
*Not enough price samples to justify a reliable range.

Baby Phyllis/11" tall / Original clothes (Emily Manning)

Baby Sandy

MAKER: Ralph Freundlich
DATE: 1939 - 1942
MATERIAL: All composition
SIZE: 7-26"
MARK: Head - "Baby Sandy"
Pin - "The Wonder Baby
Genuine Baby Sandy Doll"

Marked Baby Sandy: All composition with swivel head, jointed shoulders and hips. Chubby toddler body. Molded hair, smiling face. Larger sizes have sleep eyes, smaller ones painted eyes. Appropriate clothes. All in good condition.

Size	7-8"	$65-75
	14-17"	$85-100

"Baby Sandy"
16"
All original with button
(Rosemary Dent)

Baby Snooks
(Ideal)

MAKER: Ideal Novelty & Toy Co., New York, N.Y., U.S.A.
DATE: 1938 - 1939
MATERIAL: Head, torso, hands and feet of composition; arms and legs made of flexible metal cable.
SIZE: 12-1/2 inches
MARK: Round tag hanging on doll reads: "FLEXY -- an Ideal Doll, Fanny Brices Baby Snooks"; head embossed "Ideal Doll"

Baby Snooks Doll: Doll described above complete with tag, dressed in original pajama-type suit; all in good condition.

Size 12-1/2" $100-125

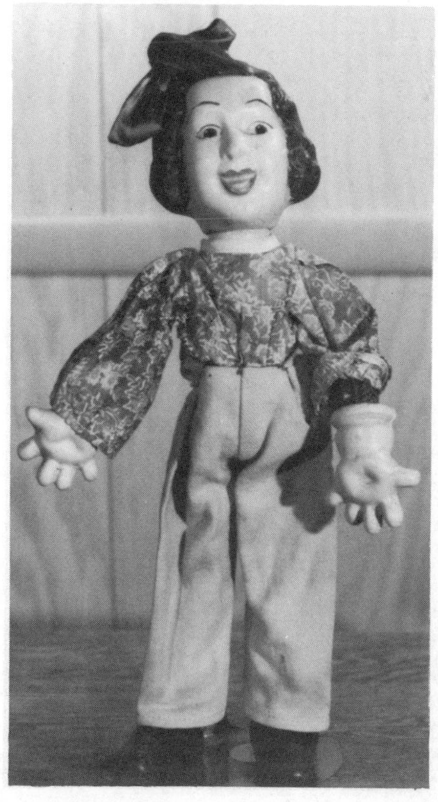

Baby Snooks
12-1/2" tall
(Bertha Neumyer)

Bähr & Pröschild Characters

MAKER: Bähr & Pröschild
DATE: 1910 - on
MATERIAL: Bisque head, composition bent-limb baby or toddler body
SIZE: Various
MARK: BP

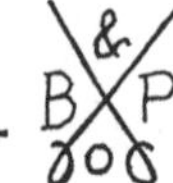

with "Germany" and numbers 585, 604, 624

Marked B.P. Character: Bisque socket head, sleep eyes, open mouth, good wig, composition bent-limb baby body; dressed; all in good condition.

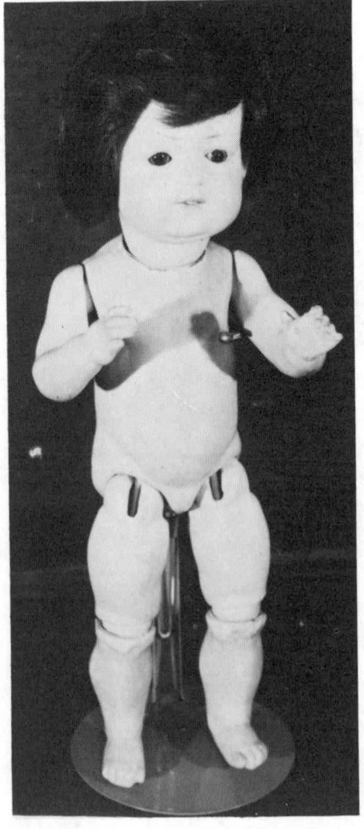

15 - 17" $250-350
depending on quality

* Allow extra for toddler body
* Allow extra for open/closed mouth

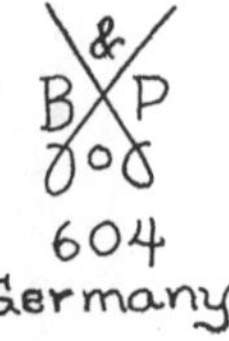

15" tall
(H & J Foulke)

Bartenstein
(Two-faced Wax)

MAKER: Fritz Bartenstein, Thüringia, Germany
DATE: 1880 - 1898
MATERIAL: Wax over composition head with two faces (crying and smiling), cardboard torso, lower limbs of composition
SIZE: Various
MARK: "Bartenstein" in purple ink, U.S. Patent #243, 752 - July 5, 1881

Bartenstein Doll: Wax over composition head, double-faced, glass eyes, permanent-type cap, body as above. Old clothes. In good condition.

15" $700-750

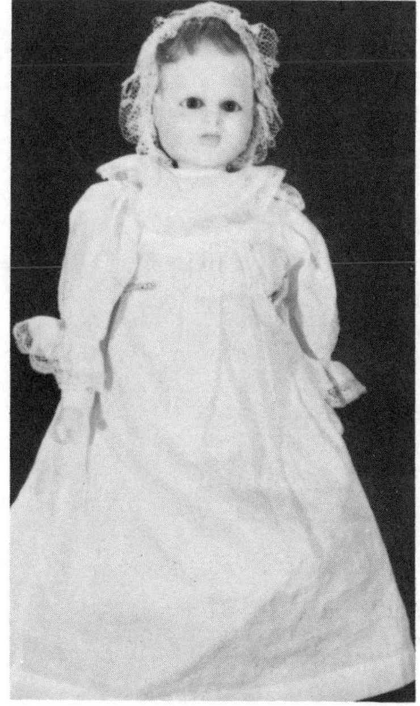

Left: Bartenstein
15" tall
(Emily Manning)

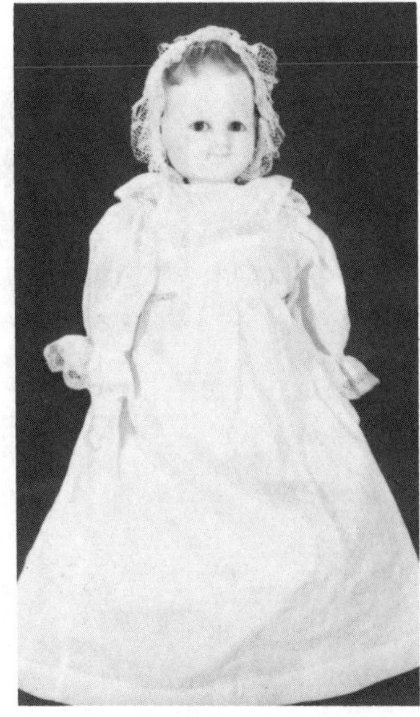

Right: Bartenstein
Smiling face

Bathing Beauty

MAKER: Various German firms
DATE: 1920's
MATERIAL: All bisque
SIZE: Up to about 7" tall or long
MARK: Sometimes "Germany" and/or numbers

Bathing Beauty: All bisque ladies, either nude or partially dressed in painted on clothing; in various sitting, lying or standing positions. Also may be dressed in bits of lace. Painted features and molded hair possibly with bathing cap (sometimes a bald head with a wig).

Ordinary poses: Size 3-4" $35-40
Standing: Size 7" $100-125

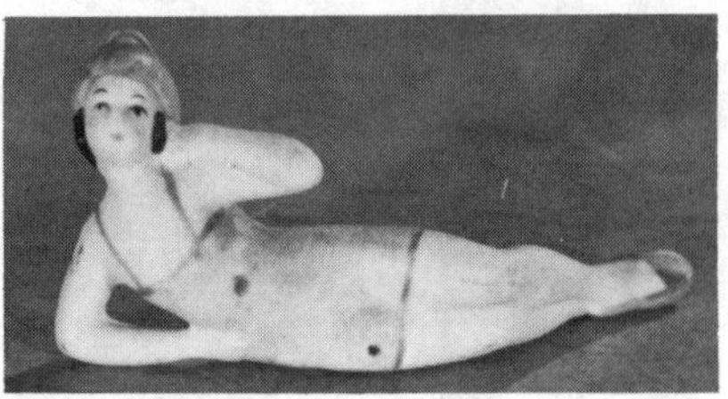

Unmarked
Bathing Beauty
3-1/2" long
(Helen Teske)

Belton-type Child
(So-called)

MAKER: Various French and German firms
DATE: Ca. 1880's
MATERIAL: Bisque socket head, ball-jointed composition body with straight wrists
SIZE: Various
MARK: None

Belton-type Child Doll: Bisque socket head, solid but flat on top with 2 or 3 small holes, paperweight eyes, closed mouth, pierced ears; composition ball-jointed body with straight wrists; dressed; all in good condition.

Size 11-13" $375-425

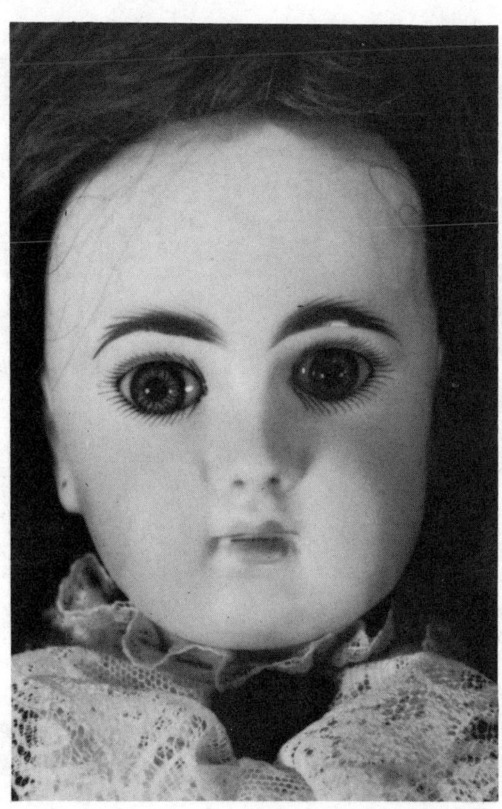

Belton-type flat top with 3 holes
Composition body
16-1/2" tall
(Richard Wright)

Bergmann Child Doll

MAKER: C.M. Bergmann of Waltershausen, Thüringia, Germany
DATE: Ca. 1889 - well into the 1900's
MATERIAL: Bisque head, composition ball-jointed body
SIZE: Various
MARK: C.M. BERGMANN / 4/0 — C.M. Bergmann / Waltershausen / Germany / 1916 / 6½a

Bergmann Child Doll: Marked bisque head, composition ball-jointed body, sleep or set eyes, open mouth, good wig, dressed. All in nice condition.

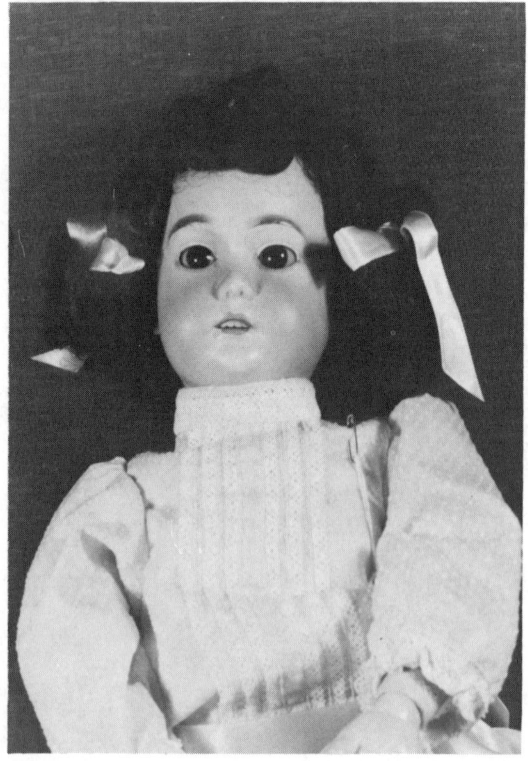

22-24" $175-200
28-31" $275-325

S&H "CMB Germany"
24" tall
(H&J Foulke)

Bisque Molded Hair

(Tinted Bisque)

MAKER: Various German firms
DATE: Last quarter 19th century
MATERIAL: Tinted bisque shoulder head; kid or cloth body
SIZE: Various
MARK: None

Molded Hair Doll: Tinted bisque shoulder head with beautifully molded hair (usually blond), painted eyes, closed mouth, original kid or cloth body, appropriate clothes; all in good condition.

12-15" $135-165
24-25" $350-400
*Allow extra for glass eyes

Bisque Molded Hair
with bangs
25" tall
Gussetted kid body
(Helen Teske)

Black Bisque Dolls

MAKER: Various German and French doll makers from their regular molds or specially designed ones with Negroid features

DATE: 1890 - on

MATERIAL: Bisque socket heads either painted dark or with dark coloring mixed in the slip of the bisque (this runs from light brown to very dark); composition body in a matching color

SIZE: Various

MARK: Various

A.M. #351 Black Baby 15-16"
$325-375

S.F.B.J. 60 Child 11-13"
$200-250

German Child 8 - 10"
5-piece body $150-200

S&H Child 14-16"
$350-400

Dolls with distinct Negroid features will be much higher in price.

Black Bisque
Kestner Girl
12" tall
(H&F Foulke)

Black Composition Dolls

MAKER: Various American doll firms
DATE: 1915 - on
MATERIAL: All composition, or composition heads, arms and legs with cloth bodies
SIZE: Various
MARK: Various

Black composition: Bent-limb baby or mama type, jointed at hips and shoulders and perhaps neck; molded hair, painted or sleep eyes; original clothes or good new ones. Some have three yarn tufts (on either side and on top.) All in good condition.

Baby 9 - 10"	$30-35
Toddler 17-19"	$65-75

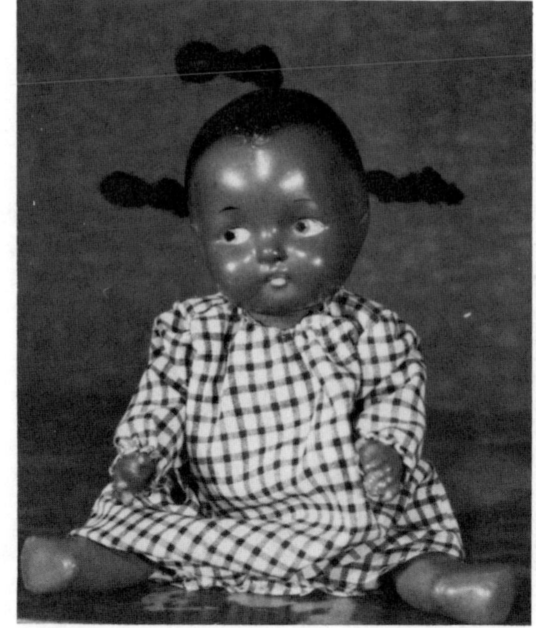

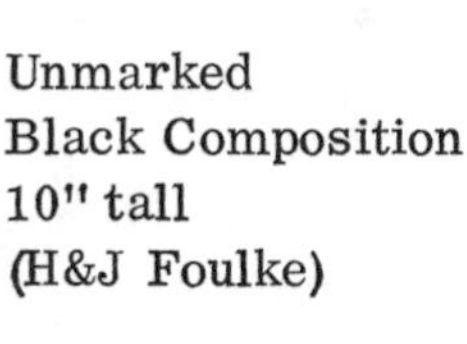

Unmarked
Black Composition
10" tall
(H&J Foulke)

Bonnet Dolls

(Bisque)

MAKER: Various German firms
DATE: Ca. 1890 to 1920
MATERIAL: Bisque shoulder heads (usually stone bisque), cloth bodies, china or stone bisque extremities
SIZE: Usually 12" and under
MARK: Some with numbers and/or "Germany"

Bonnet Doll: Bisque head with painted molded hair and molded fancy bonnet with bows, ribbons, flowers, feathers, etc.; painted eyes and facial features; original cloth body with original arms and legs; good old clothes or newly dressed; all in good condition.

8 - 11"	$125-165
13-15"	$175-225

Bisque Bonnet Doll
16" tall
(Bertha Neumyer)

Bonnie Babe
(Georgene Averill Baby)

MAKER: Heads by Alt, Beck & Gottschalck of Nauendorf, Thüringia, Germany. Cloth bodies by George Borgfeldt & Co. of New York, N.Y., U.S.A.

DATE: 1926, renewed 1946

MATERIAL: Bisque heads, cloth bodies, composition arms and legs

SIZE: Various

DESIGNER: Georgene Averill, U.S.A. (Madame Hendren)

MARK: Copr. by
Georgene Averill
Germany

Marked Bonnie Babe: Bisque head, cloth body, composition extremities, molded hair, set or sleep eyes, open mouth with two teeth; dressed; all in good condition.

Size 15-17" $600-650 Size 22-24" $750-800

All-bisque Bonnie Babe: Molded hair, open mouth with two lower teeth.Glass eyes, pink or blue molded slippers.Jointed at neck, shoulders and hips. Size 4-1/2 to 5-1/2 $550-650

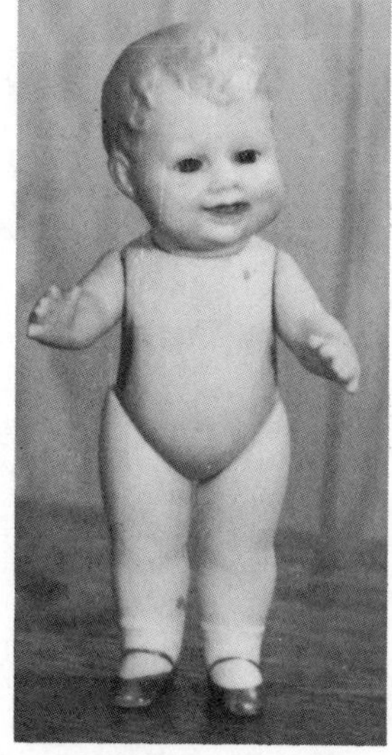

Left: Georgene Averill, Bonnie Babe, 16" tall (Bertha Neumyer)
Right: All-bisque, Bonnie Babe, 5-1/2" tall, (Bertha Neumyer)

Betty Boop

MAKER: Cameo Doll Products Co.
DATE: 1932
MATERIAL: Composition head and torso; wood segmented arms and legs.
SIZE: 12-1/2 inches
MARK: "Betty Boop" label on body

Betty Boop: Composition swivel-head, painted and molded hair, large goo-goo eyes, tiny closed mouth. Composition torso with wood segmented arms and legs. Molded on bathing suit. All in good condition. Size 11-13" $200-300

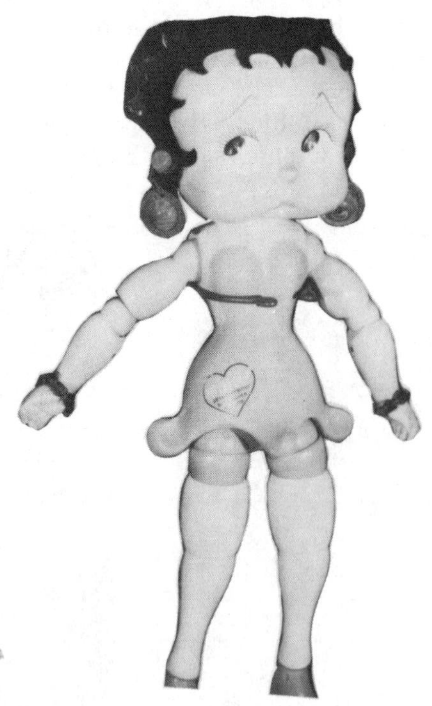

12" tall
Added earrings
(Mike White)

Boudoir Dolls

MAKER: Various French, U.S. and Italian firms
DATE: Early 1920's into the early 1930's
MATERIAL: Heads of composition and other materials; bodies mostly cloth but also of composition and other substances.
SIZE: Many 24" to 36"; some smaller
MARK: Mostly unmarked

Boudoir Doll: Composition shoulder head, painted features; composition or cloth stuffed body; unusually long extremities; usually high-heeled shoes; original clothes elaborately designed and trimmed. All in good condition.

Size 24-28" $25-35

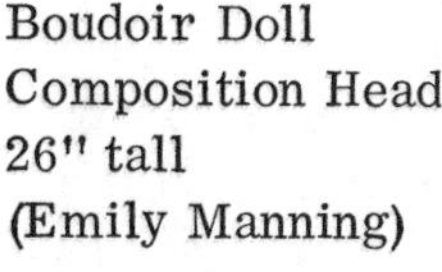

Boudoir Doll
Composition Head
26" tall
(Emily Manning)

Brū Bébé

MAKER: Bru Jne. & Cie., Paris, France
DATE: Ca. 1879 to 1899
MATERIAL: Bisque swivel shoulder head, gusseted all-kid body, sometimes wooden legs, bisque hands; or bisque socket head on jointed composition body.
SIZE: 10" and up
MARK: Incised Marks:

BRU. JNE R
11
B R U

Paper label on body:

BÉBÉ BRU BTE S.G.D.G.
Tout Contrefacteur sera saisiet poursuivi conformement ala Loi

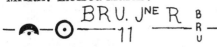

Marked Bru Bébé: Bisque head on body as above, beautiful wig, set blown glass eyes, closed mouth, pierced ears; lovely clothes. All in good condition.

Kid body, closed mouth. Size 20-24" $3000 up
Composition body, closed mouth. Size 21" $2800 up
Composition body, open mouth. Size 21" $1700 up

Left: "Bru Jne", 10, Composition body, 22" tall (Bertha Neumyer)
Right: Kid body, Black Bru, 17" tall (Richard Wright)

Bru Nursing Doll

(Bébé Teteur)

MAKER: Bru Jne. & Cie., Paris, France
DATE: Ca. 1879 - 1899
MATERIAL: Bisque head, lower arms and hands, kid body. Upper arm and upper legs of metal covered with kid. Lower legs of carved wood; or jointed composition body
SIZE: Various
MARK: "BRU", "BRU JNE", "BÉBÉ BRU" etc.

Marked Nursing Bru: Bisque head on shoulder plate, original or lovely replacement wig, beautiful set eyes, open/closed mouth with hole for nipple, kid body as above. Good clothing. All in good condition.

15-20" $2,000-2,400
SFBJ model 13-16"
$1,250-1,650

Nursing SFBJ Bru
Composition Body
15-16" tall
(Emily Manning)

Brückner Rag Doll

MAKER: Albert Brückner, Jersey City, N.J., U.S.A.
DATE: 1901 - on
MATERIAL: All cloth with stiffened mask face
SIZE: About 13 - 15"
MARK: On right front shoulder: PAT'D. JULY 8TH 1901

Marked Brückner: Cloth head with printed features on stiffened mask face. Cloth body flexible at shoulders and hips. Appropriate clothes. All in good condition.

13-15" $50-65

Also made a "Topsy Turvy" black and white doll 13-15" $95-115

Left: Bruckner/"Pat'd July 2nd 1901"; 13" tall (Joan Kindler)
Right: Close view of same doll

Bubbles
(EFFanBEE)

MAKER: EFFanBEE Doll Corporation (Fleischaker & Baum) New York, N.Y., U.S.A.
DATE: 1924 - on
MATERIAL: Composition head and arms, cloth body, cloth or composition legs.
SIZE: Various
MARK: "EFFanBEE BUBBLES 1924" or "EFFanBEE DOLLS WALK, TALK, SLEEP. Made in U.S.A." also a tag on wrist printed "This is BUBBLES".

Marked Bubbles: Composition head with blond molded painted hair, open mouth, sleep eyes, cloth body, curved composition arms and legs. Appropriate clothes. All in good condition.

16-20" $55-65*
*Allow extra for straight legs.

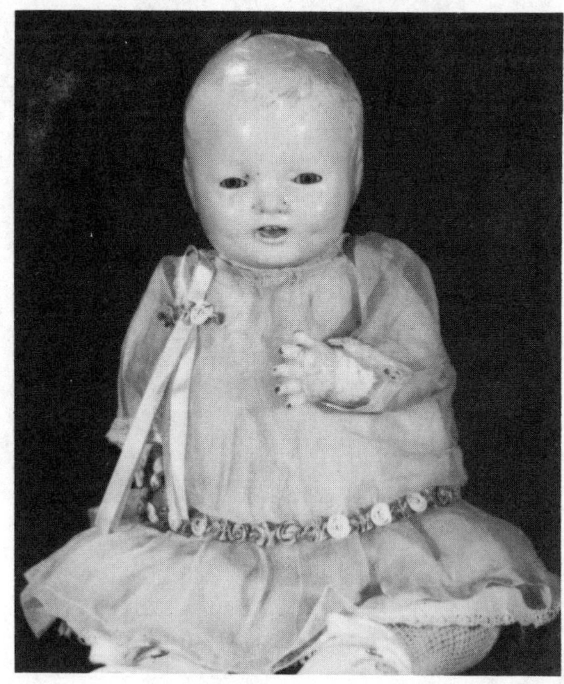

Bubbles
15" tall
(Emily Manning)

Butch

MAKER: Alexander Doll Co., New York, N.Y., U.S.A.
DATE: 1942
MATERIAL: Composition head and limbs; cloth torso
SIZE: 11" - 18"
MARK: "Alexander" on head; "Butch" on clothes tag

Butch: Composition swivel head with lashed sleep eyes, closed mouth, soft mohair wig; soft body with composition hands and legs; original clothes; all in good condition. Size 11" $45-55
Size 18" $75-85

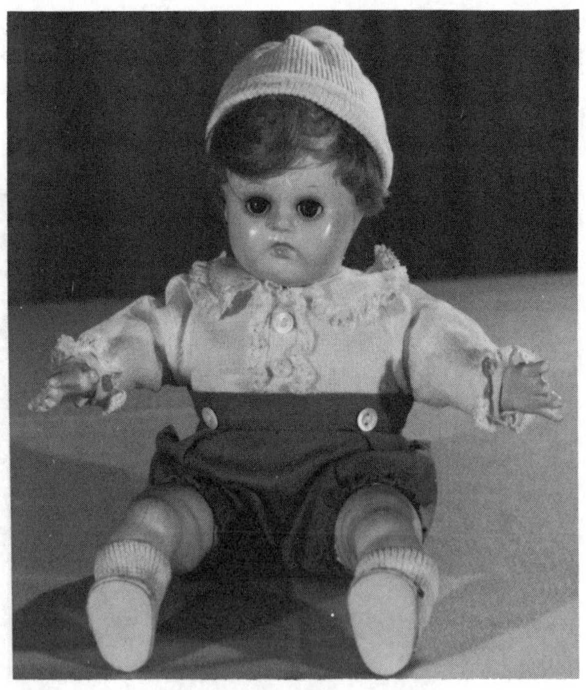

Butch
11" tall
All original
(Barbara Crescenze)

Bye-lo Baby
(Composition Head)

MAKER: Cameo Doll Co., New York, N.Y., U.S.A. (Composition heads only)
DATE: 1924 - on
MATERIAL: Composition head, cloth body
SIZE: Various
DESIGNER: Grace Storey Putnam, U.S.A.
MARK: "GRACE STOREY PUTNAM"

Marked BYE-LO BABY: Composition head, cloth body, sleep eyes, composition hands, nice clothes.

Size 12-13" $145-165

Bye-lo with Composition head 17" long (Clendenien Collection)

Bye-lo Baby

(All Bisque)

MAKER: J.D. Kestner, Waltershausen, Thüringia, Germany
DATE: 1925 - on
MATERIAL: All bisque
SIZE: Up to 8"
DESIGNER: Grace S. Putnam
MARK: Dark green paper label on front torso(often missing)

Marked Bye-Lo: All bisque with molded hair and painted eyes, jointed shoulders and hips.

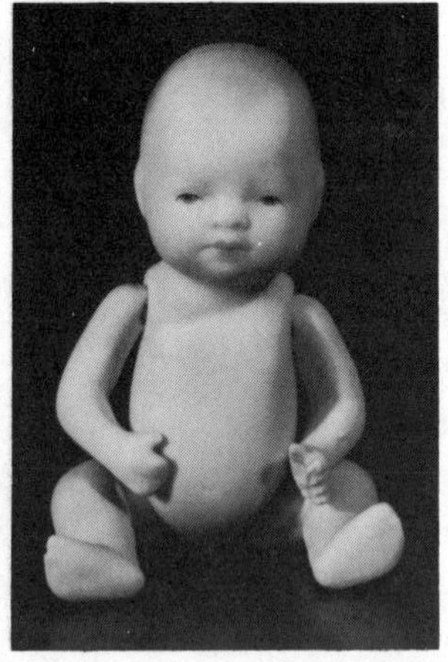

4"	$210-235
4-5"	$425-475*

*(with glass eyes and wig)

"20-10
Cpr by/Grace S. Putnam/
Germany"
4" tall
(H&J Foulke)

Bye-lo Baby

(Bisque Head)

MAKER: Heads - J.D. Kestner of Waltershausen, Thüringia, Germany; Alt, Beck & Gottschalck of Nauendorf, Thüringia; C.F. Kling & Co. of Ohrdruf, Thüringia; Hertel, Schwab & Co. of Luisenthal near Ohrdruf, Thüringia. Bodies - K & K Toy Co. of New York, N.Y., U.S.A.

DATE: 1923 - on

MATERIAL: Bisque head, cloth body, celluloid or composition hands

SIZE: Seven sizes from 9" to 20"

DESIGNER: Grace Storey Putnam (both head and body), U.S.A.

MARK: "BYE-LO BABY" on body, "GRACE S. PUTNAM" on head; some dated 1923

Marked Bye-Lo Baby: Fine condition, bisque head, cloth body, celluloid hands, sleep eyes, dressed.

8 - 10" $250-325
12-13" $350-395
14-15" $425-450

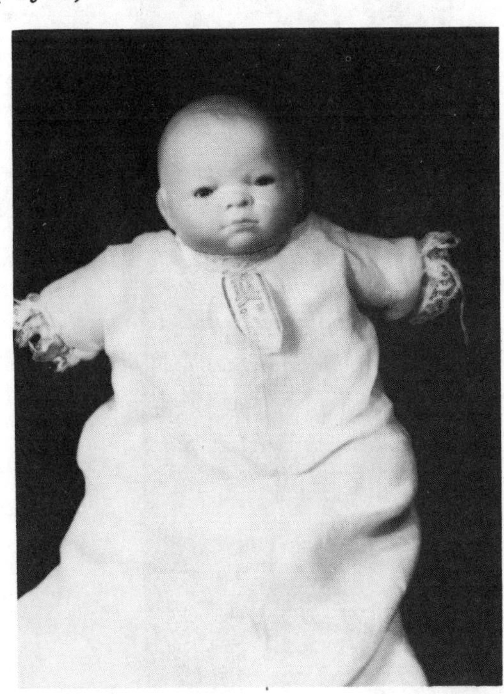

© 1923 by
Grace S. Putnam
Made in Germany
Original dress
with Label
(H&J Foulke)

C.O.D. Doll
(Dressel)

MAKER: Cuno & Otto Dressel of Sonneberg, Thüringia, Germany
DATE: Ca. 1895 - on
MATERIAL: Bisque shoulder head, jointed kid or cloth body; bisque socket head, ball-jointed composition body
SIZE: Various
MARK: "C & O Dressel - Germany", "C O D", sometimes Mark reproduced below

---

C O D DOLL: Marked bisque head, original jointed kid or composition body, good wig, glass eyes, open mouth, suitable clothes; all in good condition.

14-15" $135-145
16-18" $150-160
20-24" $165-195

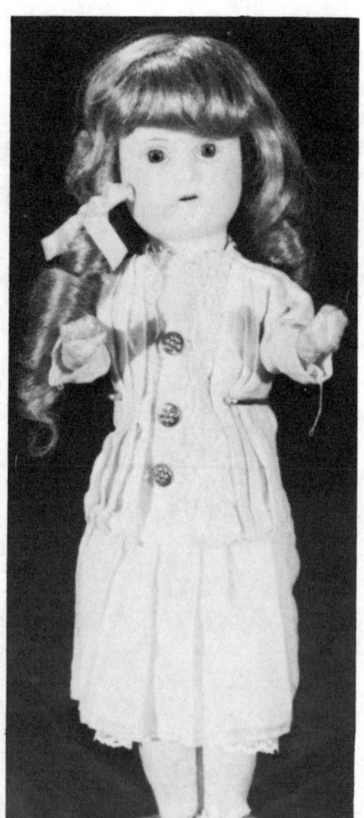

"C.O.D."
13" tall
(Emily Manning)

C.O.D. Lady Doll

MAKER: Cuno & Otto Dressel of Sonneberg, Thüringia, Germany
DATE: Ca. 1920's
MATERIAL: Bisque socket head, jointed composition body
SIZE: About 14 inches
MARK: "C.O.D. Germany"

COD Lady: Bisque socket head with young lady face, good wig, sleeping eyes, closed mouth; jointed composition body in adult form with molded bust, slim waist and long arms and legs, feet modeled to wear high-heeled shoes. Appropriate clothes. All in good condition. Size 13-14" $400

COD Lady
14" tall
(Bertha Neumyer)

Campbell Kid

MAKER: E.I. Horsman Co., Inc., New York, N.Y., U.S.A.
DATE: 1948
MATERIAL: All composition
SIZE: 12 - 12-1/2"
DESIGNER: Grace G. Drayton
MARK: None

Campbell Kid: All composition with molded, painted hair, painted eyes to side, watermelon mouth. Painted white socks and black slippers. Original clothes. All in good condition.

12" $75-85

Campbell Kid
Original dress
12" tall
(H&J Foulke)

Campbell Kid
(Horsman)

MAKER: E.I. Horsman Co., Inc., New York, N.Y., U.S.A.
DATE: 1910 to 1914
MATERIAL: Composition head and arms, cloth body and legs
SIZE: Usually 10-15"
DESIGNER: Grace G. Drayton
MARK: E.I.H. © 1910

Campbell Kid: Marked composition head with flange neck, painted features, original cloth body, composition arms, cloth legs and feet, original romper suit, all in nice condition.

10-12" $65-75

Campbell Kid
15" tall
(Bertha Neumyer)

Candy Kid

(EFFanBEE)

MAKER: Fleischaker & Baum, New York, N.Y., U.S.A.
DATE: 1946
MATERIAL: All composition
SIZE: 13 inches
MARK: "Effanbee" on head and torso EFF AND BEE

Candy Kid: All composition toddler, jointed at neck, shoulders and hips; molded hair, sleep eyes. Original clothes. All in good condition. 12" $50-60

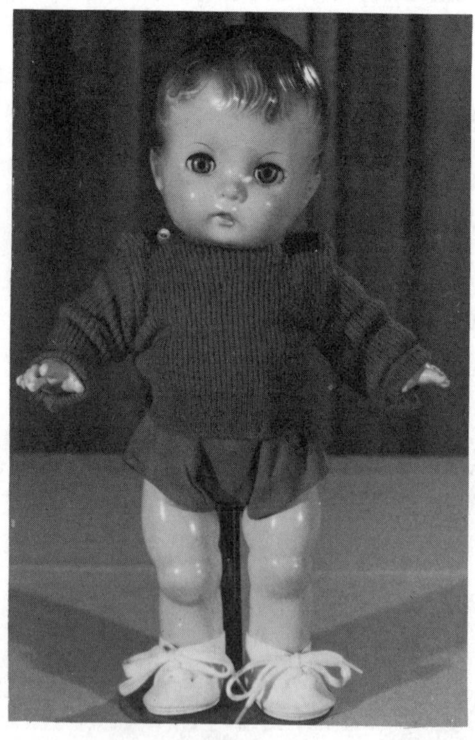

"Candy Kid" 13" tall
Original clothes
(Barbara Crescenze)

Celluloid Dolls

MAKERS: Rheinische Gummi und Celluloid Fabrik Co. Mannheim-Neckarau, Bavaria, Germany and Buschow & Beck, Silesia and Saxony, Germany
DATE: These dolls from 1899 to perhaps the 1920's or later
MATERIAL: All celluloid
SIZE: Various
MARK: Embossed turtle mark with or without the diamond frame; sometimes "SCHUTZ MARKE" and "Made in Germany"

All celluloid, Marked: Bent-limb baby, painted eyes, molded hair, jointed arms and/or legs, closed mouth; no clothes; all in good condition. Size 6" $15-20
Child doll as above: 4-6" $10-15, (original clothes) 9-10" $25-35
Child doll, glass eyes, wig, jointed neck, shoulders, and hips. Dressed. All in good condition. Size 18" $60-75

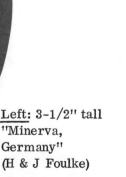

Right: 18" tall
Turtle Mark
Flirty eyes
(H & J Foulke)

Left: 3-1/2" tall
"Minerva, Germany"
(H & J Foulke)

Celluloid-Head Dolls

(Kid, Cloth or Composition Body)

MAKER: Rheinische Gummi und Celluloid Fabrik Co., Mannheim-Neckarau, Bavaria, Germany

DATE: 1869 - on

MATERIAL: Celluloid head; jointed kid, cloth or composition body

SIZE: Various

MARK: Embossed turtle mark with or without the diamond frame; sometimes "SCHUTZ MARKE" and "Made in Germany". Also made celluloid heads from molds of Kestner and Kammer & Reinhart whose marks also appear on the heads.

Marked Celluloid Head: Celluloid shoulder head, glass eyes (set) and wig; open or closed mouth, celluloid or composition arms, dressed; all in good condition. On a cloth body or kid body. 12-14" $50-75

Celluloid socket head, glass eyes (sometimes flirty) and wig, open mouth, composition body (ball-jointed or bent-limb); dressed; all in good condition.

18-22"	$125-150
24-25"	$175-185

Celluloid Head
Glass eyes and wig
Composition body
21" tall
(Emily Manning)

Century Infant Doll

MAKER: Century Doll Co., New York, N.Y., U.S.A.; bisque heads by J.D. Kestner, Germany

DATE: Ca. 1925

MATERIAL: Bisque head, cloth body, composition arms (and legs)

SIZE: Various

MARK: "Century Doll Co." Sometimes  or Kestner "Germany"

Marked Century Infant: Bisque solid dome head, molded and painted sleep eyes, closed or open-closed mouth; cloth body, composition hands or limbs, dressed; all in good condition.

Size 12-15" $250-300

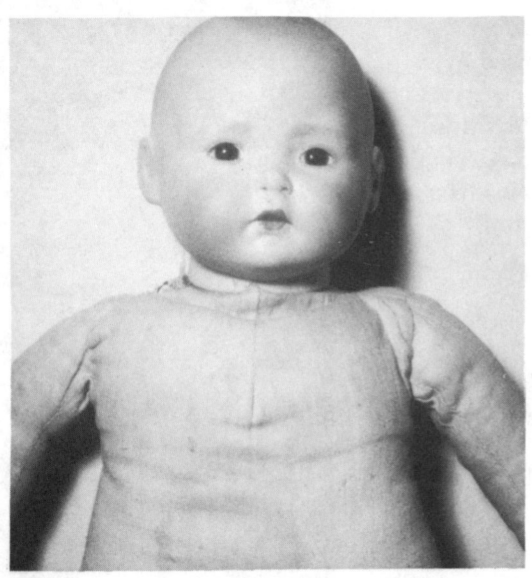

Century Baby (May Wenzel)

Chad Valley

MAKER: Chad Valley Co. (formerly Johnson Bros., Ltd.)
Birmingham, England
DATE: 1923 - on
MATERIAL: All cloth
SIZE: Various
MARK: Paper or cloth label

Chad Valley Doll: All cloth, usually velvet body; jointed neck, shoulders and hips. Mohair wig, glass or painted eyes. Original clothes. All in good condition.

13-15" painted eyes $55-75
16-18" child, glass eyes $85-125
15" Royal children $150-200

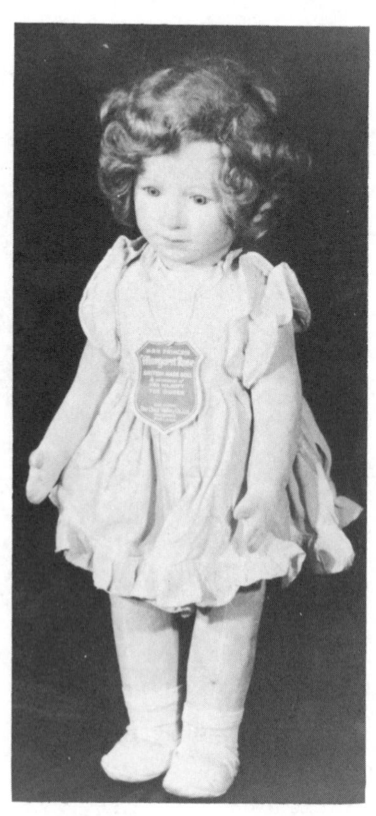

Chad Valley "Princess Margaret Rose"
All original
16" tall
(Richard Wright)

Charlie Chaplin

MAKER: Louis Amberg & Son, New York, N.Y., U.S.A.
DATE: 1915
MATERIAL: Composition head and hands; straw-filled cloth body
SIZE: 13"
MARK: Cloth label "Charlie Chaplin
World's Greatest Comedian"

Charlie Chaplin: Composition head with molded and painted hair, painted eyes to side, closed, full mouth. Cloth body with composition hands. Original clothes. All in good condition. 13" $150-200

For photo see DOLLS, IMAGES OF LOVE, p. 103

Chase Stockinet

MAKER: Martha Jenks Chase, Pawtucket, Rhode Island, U.S.A.
DATE: 1891 to ca. 1951 (play doll)
MATERIAL: Stockinet and cloth, painted in oils
SIZE: 9" to life size
DESIGNER: Martha Jenks Chase
MARK: "Chase Stockinet Doll" on left leg or under left arm, paper label on back (usually gone)

PAWTUCKET, R.I
MADE IN U.S.A.

Chase Doll: Head and limbs of stockinet, treated and painted with oils. Rough-stroked hair to provide texture. Cloth bodies jointed at shoulders, hips, elbows and knees; later ones only at shoulders and hips. Not in perfect condition.

Size 16-20" $150-195*
Size 24-28" $225-275*

*Allow extra for rare bobbed hair with bangs.

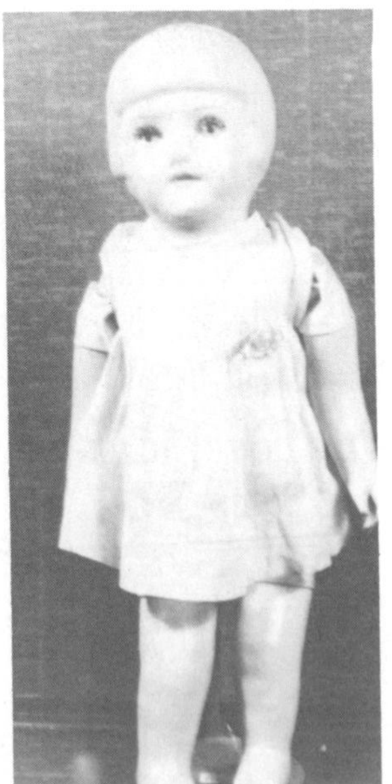

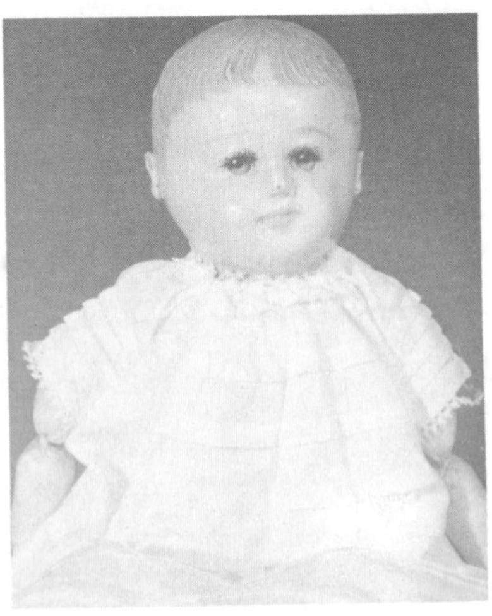

Left: Chase girl, Dutch-cut bobbed hair, 12-1/2" tall, ca. 1922
Right: Chase baby with early jointed elbows and knees, 17" tall, both dolls from H & J Foulke

China Head

(Exposed Ears, Short Curly Hair)

MAKER: Unknown German firms
DATE: 1880's
MATERIAL: Cloth body; china arms and legs
SIZE: Various
MARK: None

Short Curly Hair, Exposed Ears: Black-or-blond-haired china shoulder head, blue painted eyes, old cloth body, china arms and legs; dressed; all in good condition.

16-20" $175-200*
*often dressed as a boy

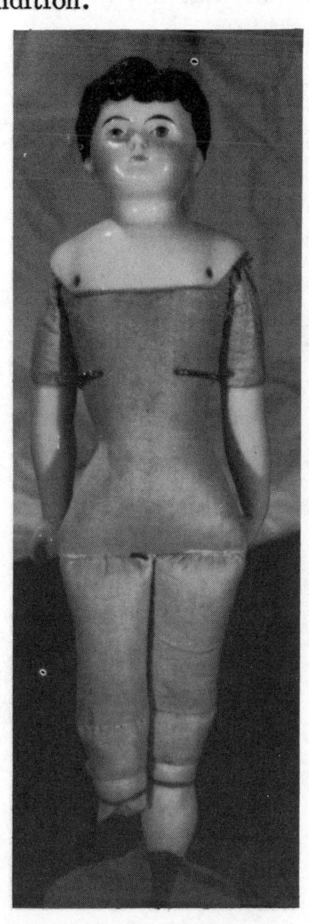

"Exposed Ears"
China
12" tall
(Emily Manning)

China Head Doll "Bald"

(Biedermeier - So-called)

MAKER: Unknown German firms
DATE: 1840's thru the early 1900's
MATERIAL: Bald china shoulder head, some with black areas on top of head; cloth body, bisque, china or leather arms
SIZE: Various
MARK: None

"BALD" China Doll: China shoulder head, blue painted eyes, proper wig, kid arms, old cloth body, nice dress; all in good condition. 14 - 18" $450-475

Left: "Bald" China
13" tall
(Bertha Neumyer)

Right: Same doll
showing black pate

China Head Doll - "Bangs"

MAKER: Unknown German firms
DATE: 1880's thru 1890's
MATERIAL: China shoulder head on cloth or kid body
SIZE: Various
MARK: Some marked "Germany"

"BANG" China Doll: Black or blond-haired china shoulder head, bangs on forehead, original cloth or kid body, leather arms, blue painted eyes, old china legs, dressed; all in good condition. 16 - 18" $200-250

China Head with Bangs
19" tall
(Emily Manning)

China Head Doll-"Common"

(Also Called Low Brow)

MAKER: Unknown German firms
DATE: 1880's to 1940
MATERIAL: China shoulder head, cloth or kid body; stub, leather, bisque or china limbs
SIZE: Various
MARK: Some with numbers and/or "Germany"

"COMMON" China Head Doll: Black or blond wavy hair style as pictured; blue painted eyes, old body, old limbs, original or good clothes; all in good condition.

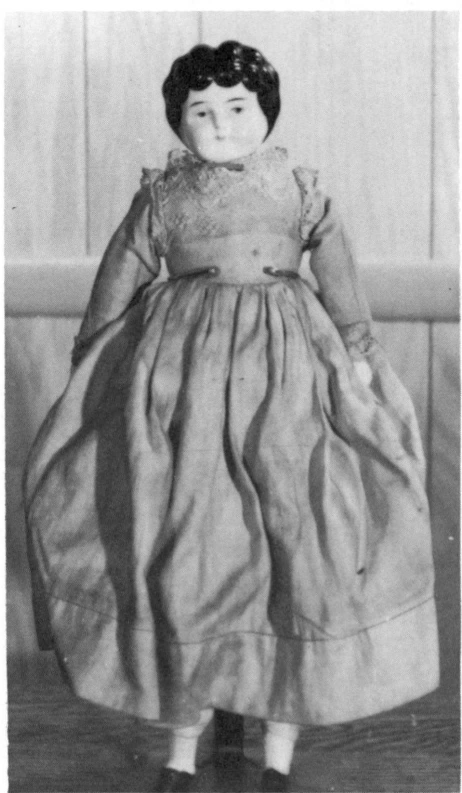

7-10" $35-50
14-16" $75-90
20-22" $125-150

Common China Head
16" tall
(Bertha Neumyer)

China Head - "Covered Wagon"

MAKER: Unknown German firms
DATE: 1840 to 1870
MATERIAL: China shoulder head, cloth body, varied extremities
SIZE: Various
MARK: None

"COVERED WAGON" Doll: Black-haired china shoulder head, pink tint, blue painted eyes, old cloth body, arms and legs; very well dressed; all in good condition.

14-18" $300-325

"Covered Wagon" China Head
7" tall
(Emily Manning)

China Head - "Dolley Madison"

MAKER: Unknown German firms
DATE: 1875 to 1895
MATERIAL: China shoulder head, cloth body, leather arms
SIZE: Various
MARK: None

"DOLLEY MADISON" China Doll: Black-haired china shoulder head, molded ribbon bow in front and molded band on back of head; painted blue eyes, beautiful clothes, original cloth body, leather arms and boots; entire doll in fine condition.

15 - 20" $175-225

"Dolley Madison"
China Head
17" tall
All original
(Emily Manning)

China Head - "Flat Top"

MAKER: Unknown German firms
DATE: Late 1850 thru late 1870
MATERIAL: China shoulder head, cloth body; extremities leather or china
SIZE: Various
MARK: None

"FLAT TOP" China Doll: China shoulder head with black hair, old cloth body, painted blue eyes, leather arms and boots or china limbs, old clothes or newly well costumed; all in good condition.

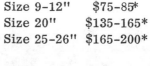

Size 9-12"	$75-85*
Size 20"	$135-165*
Size 25-26"	$165-200*

*Allow extra for pink tone or for brown eyes.

Flat-top China
18" tall
All original
(Emily Manning)

China Head Doll-"K" in Bell

(Kling & Co.)

MAKER: Kling & Co. of Ohrdruf, Thüringia, Germany
DATE: 1880's to 1900
MATERIAL: China shoulder head, cloth body, bisque or china limbs
SIZE: Various
MARK: [bell with K] and sometimes "Germany"

Marked "Kling" China Doll: Pink tinted black or blond-haired china head, old cloth body, original arms and legs; lovely costume; all in good condition.

12 - 16" $100-150

Kling-type China Head
15" tall
(Mildred Scheer)

China Head - "Pet Name"

MAKER: Hertwig & Co. of Katzhütte, Thüringia; and/or Closter Veilsdorf, Thüringia, Germany
DATE: 1905 - on
MATERIAL: China shoulder head, cloth body - some with printed alphabet or other figures printed on cotton material; china limbs
SIZE: Various
NAMES: "AGNES", "BERTHA", "DAISY", "DOROTHY", "EDITH", "ESTHER", "ETHEL", "FLORENCE", "HELEN", "MABEL", "MARION", "PAULINE", etc.
MARK: Some with "Germany"

"Pet Name" China Doll: China shoulder head, molded yoke with name, black or blond painted hair (one-third were blond); painted blue eyes; old cloth body, good old limbs, dressed properly; all in good condition.

7-10" $55-65
15-20" $85-125
24-27" $150-200

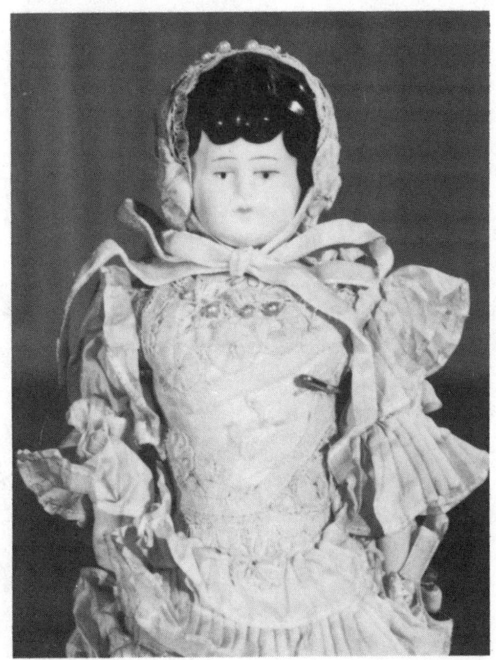

China marked "Ethel"
13" tall
(Joyce Alderson)

China Head - "Snood"

MAKER: Unknown German firms
DATE: 1860's and 1870's
MATERIAL: China shoulder head with molded snood in hair; cloth or kid body, limbs varied but often of leather
SIZE: Various
MARK: None

"SNOOD" China Head Doll: Black painted hair, slender features, painted blue eyes, molded eyelids, gold-colored snood, deep shoulders, 3 sew holes, cloth body with old china arms; beautifully gowned; all in nice condition. Size 17-20" $350*

*Not enough price samples to justify a reliable range.

China head with
Molded gold snood
14" tall
Original clothes
(Emily Manning)

Chubby Kid-type

DISTRIBUTORS: Various American firms
DATE: 1913 - on
MATERIAL: All composition
SIZE: 11" - 13"
MARK: Various, many also unmarked

Chubby Kid-type: All composition, one piece with jointed arms, often on a round base. Painted eyes and features. Molded hair or mohair wig. Undressed. In good condition.

Size 12-13" $30-45

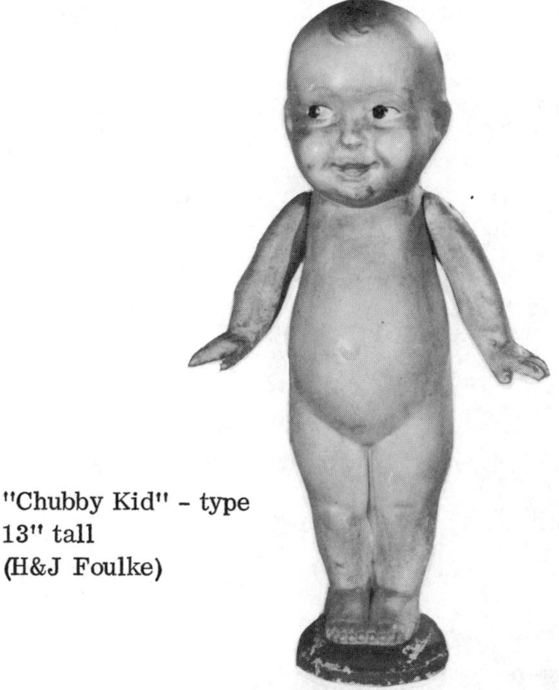

"Chubby Kid" - type
13" tall
(H&J Foulke)

Clear Dolls

MAKER: Emma Clear, Redondo Beach, Ca., U.S.A.
DATE: 1940's - on
MATERIAL: Porcelain heads, glazed or unglazed, cloth bodies
SIZES: Various
MARK: Clear and date

Signed Clear doll: Shoulder head with molded hair and painted eyes, beautiful porcelain, exquisitely modeled, lovely decoration. Cloth bodies.

Most Models: Size 18-22" $200-250
George & Martha Washington: Size 19-20" $700 pair

Emma Clear
1946
22" tall
(Bertha Neumyer)

Clowns

MAKER: Various French and German firms
DATE: 1890 - on
MATERIAL: Bisque or papier-mâché head, composition body
SIZE: Usually small
MARK: Various

Clown having standard bisque head painted with clown make-up, composition body, glass eyes, open mouth, wig, clown costume. 7-10" $100-150

Clown with molded bisque smiling face, painted or glass eyes, molded hair or wig, clown paint on face, composition body, clown costume. 12-13" $500 up

Same as second description above with molded papier-mâché head. 11-13" $150-175

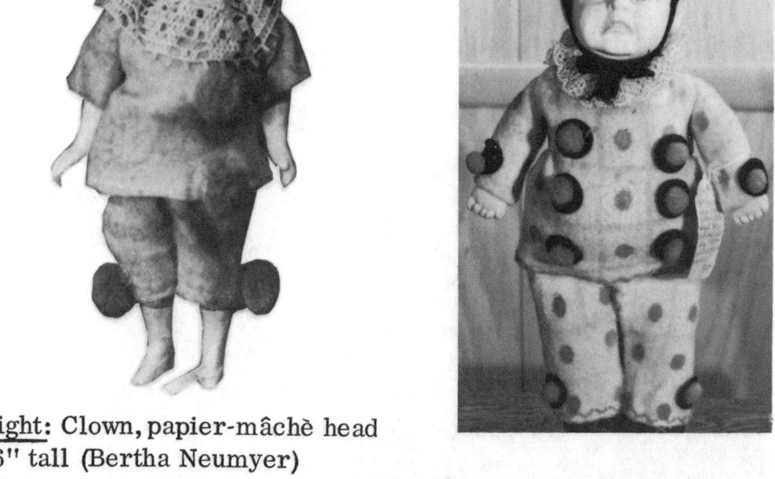

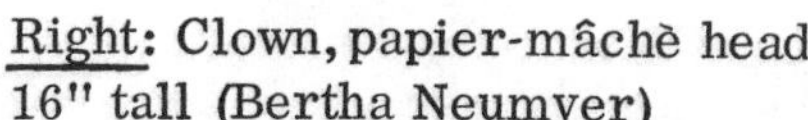

Right: Clown, papier-mâchè head 16" tall (Bertha Neumyer)

Left: Clown, standard bisque head, 6-1/2" (H&J Foulke)

Dewees Cochran

MAKER: Dewees Cochran, Fenton, Ca., U.S.A.
DATE: 1945 - on
MATERIAL: Latex and ceramic flour
SIZE: 9" - 17"
MARK: Signed under arm

Signed Dewees Cochran: Doll entirely of latex with jointed neck, shoulders and hips; human hair wig, painted eyes, character face; dressed; all in good condition. 13-15" $175-275

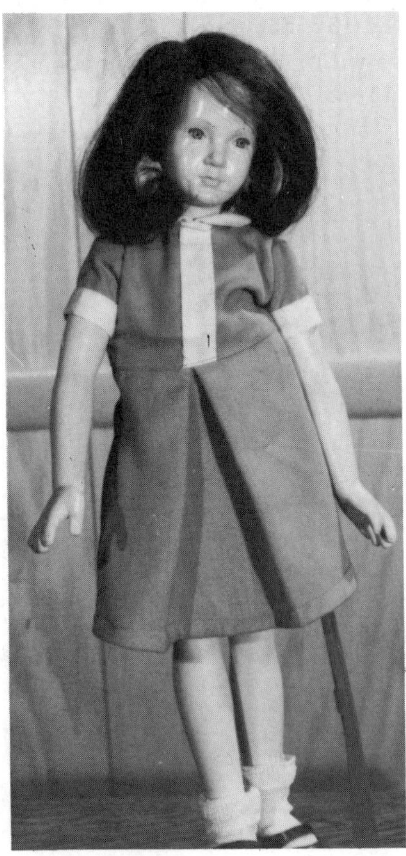

Signed Dewees Cochran
17" tall
(Bertha Neumyer)

Columbian Doll

MAKER: Emma and Marietta Adams
DATE: 1891 - 1910 or later
MATERIAL: All cloth
SIZE: 15" - 29"
MARK: Before 1900 - COLUMBIAN DOLL
EMMA E. ADAMS
OSWEGO CENTRE
N.Y.
After 1906 - THE COLUMBIAN DOLL
MANUFACTURED BY
MARIETTA ADAMS RUTTAN
OSWEGO, N.Y.

Columbian Doll: All cloth with hair and features hand painted, treated limbs; appropriate clothes; all in good condition showing wear.

Unmarked $150*
Marked $300*

*Not enough price samples to justify a reliable range.

Columbian Doll
20" tall
(Clendenien Collection)

Composition Shoulder Head
(19th Century)

MAKER: Various German firms
DATE: 1880 - 1910
MATERIAL: Composition shoulder head, cloth body, composition lower limbs
SIZE: Various
MARK: None

Composition Shoulder Head: Good quality composition, glass paperweight eyes, closed or open mouth, mohair or skin wig. Cloth body with composition arms and lower legs, sometimes with molded boots. All in good condition. 12-14" $95-125
16-21" $150-200

Unmarked Composition Shoulderhead 12" tall (H&J Foulke)

DEP

MAKER: Maison Jumeau, Paris, France (Heads possibly by Simon Halbig)

DATE: Late 1890's

MATERIAL: Bisque socket head, French jointed composition body (sometimes marked Jumeau)

SIZE: About 12" - 33"

MARK: DEP and size number (up to 16 or so); sometimes stamped in red "Tête Jumeau"

DEP: Bisque socket head, sleeping eyes, painted lower lashes only, upper hair lashes (sometimes gone), open mouth, human hair wig, pierced ears. Jointed French composition body. Lovely clothes. All in good condition.

16-20" $285-325
23-26" $350-400

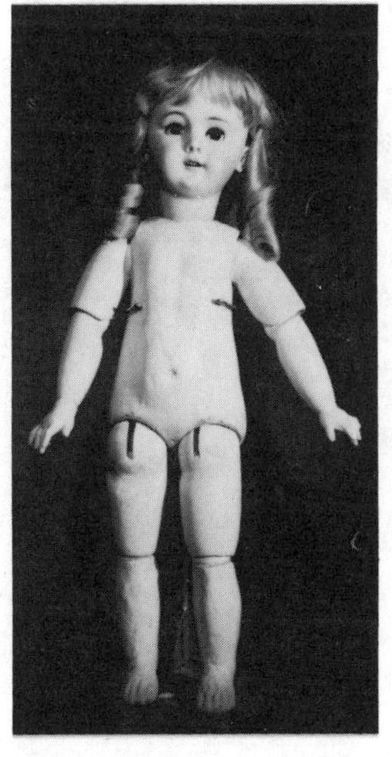

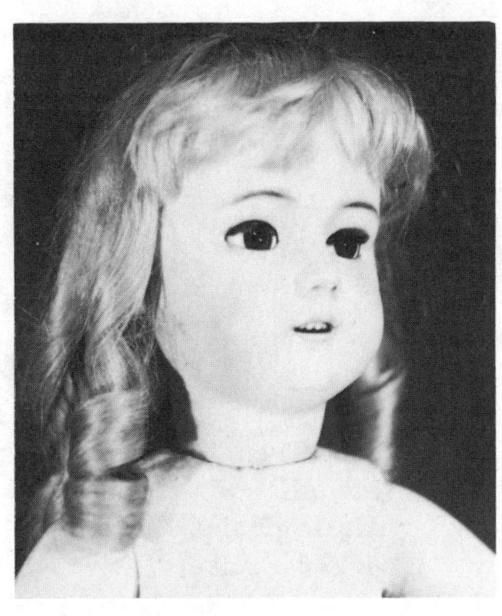

Left: "DEP"/French body; 27" tall (H&J Foulke)
Right: Same doll

Debu Teen

MAKER: Arranbee Doll Co.
DATE: Ca. 1938
MATERIAL: All composition, sometimes cloth torso
SIZE: Various
MARK: R & B on head

Debu Teen: All composition, swivel head, jointed shoulders and hips, closed mouth, lashed sleep eyes, human hair or mohair wig; original clothes; all in good condition. 15-18" $40-50

Debu Teen
14" tall
All original
(H & J Foulke)

Dionne Quintuplets

(Mme. Alexander)

MAKER: Alexander Doll Co., New York, N.Y., U.S.A.
DATE: Dec. 1935
MATERIAL: Composition; toddler or bent-limb bodies
SIZE: 7-1/2" to 20"
DESIGNER: Bernard Lipfert
MARK: "ALEXANDER"

Marked Quintuplet: All composition with original clothing, toddler or bent-limb bodies, good condition.

Size 7-1/2" $50-65
Size 10-11" $75-90
Size 14-17" $95-125

Dionne Quintuplet
Toddler
11" tall
(H & J Foulke)

Doll House Dolls

MAKER: Various German firms
DATE: Ca. 1890 to 1920
MATERIAL: Bisque shoulder head, cloth body, bisque arms and legs
SIZE: Various small sizes
MARK: Sometimes "Germany"

Doll House Doll: Man or lady 4-1/2" to 6", as above with painted eyes, molded hair, original clothes or suitably dressed; all in nice condition.

$85-125*
With glass eyes and wig $150-175*
With molded hair and painted eyes. Ca. 1920 $75
*This price includes only dolls of very good quality with old bodies and limbs.

Doll House Kitchen maid
Glass eyes, wig
5-3/4" tall
(H&J Foulke)

Dolly Walker

(Coleman Walking Doll)

MAKER. Wood Toy Co., New York, N.Y., U.S.A.
DATE: 1917 - 1923
MATERIAL: Composition head, frame torso, wood arms and legs
SIZE: 18" - 28"
DESIGNER: Harry H. Coleman
MARK: Sometimes stamped "Patented in U.S.A./other Patents Pending/Patents applied for in all other countries

---

Coleman Walker (a non-mechanical walking doll): Composition head with painted or sleeping eyes, molded hair or wig. Torso a wooden frame with wire mesh. Wooden limbs. Dressed. In good condition.

28" $75-95

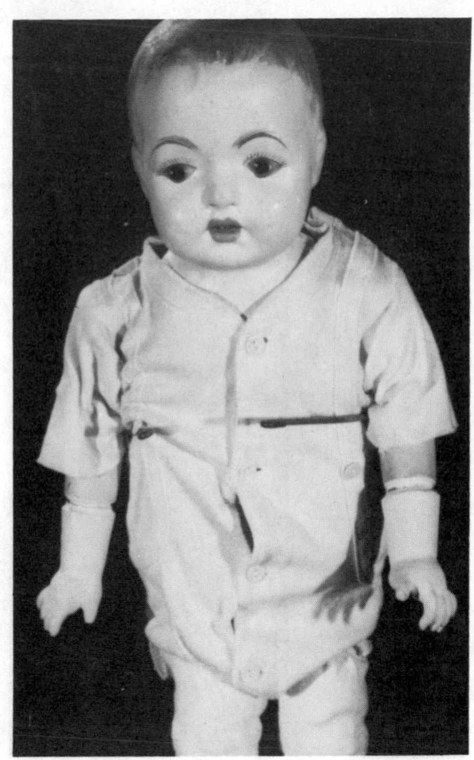

Dolly Walker
26" tall
(Emily Manning)

Door of Hope

MAKER: Door of Hope Mission, China
DATE: 1917 - on
MATERIAL: Wooden heads and hands, cloth bodies
SIZE: Various; usually under 13"
CARVER: Ning-Po
MARK: Sometimes "Made in China" label

Door of Hope: Carved wooden head with painted and/or carved hair, carved features; cloth body; sometimes carved hands. Original handmade clothes, exact costuming for different classes of Chinese people. All in good condition.

Size 11-13" $75-95

Unmarked
Door of Hope
All original
(Helen Teske)

Deanna Durbin
(Ideal)

MAKER: Ideal Novelty & Toy Co., Brooklyn, N.Y., U.S.A.
DATE: 1938
MATERIAL: Composition
SIZE: Various
MARK: "DEANNA DURBIN, IDEAL DOLL, U.S.A."

Marked Deanna Durbin: All-composition doll, jointed at neck, shoulders and hips; sleep eyes, smiling mouth with teeth. Original wig, original clothing. All in good condition.

18" $110-125

15" Deanna Durbin; All original with pin (H&J Foulke)

Dy-Dee Baby

MAKER: EFFanBEE Doll Co., New York, N.Y., U.S.A.
DATE: 1933 - on
MATERIAL: Hard rubber head, soft rubber body; later - hard plastic head
SIZE: 9" - 20"
MARK:

EFF-AN-BEE
DY-DEE BABY
US PAT.-1-857-485
ENGLAND-880-060
FRANCE-723-980
GERMANY-585-647
OTHER PAT PENDING

Marked Dy-Dee Baby: Hard rubber head with open mouth for drinking, soft ears (after 1940), caracul wig or molded hair. Soft rubber body, jointed shoulders and hips. Undressed. All in good condition. Size 11" $50-60

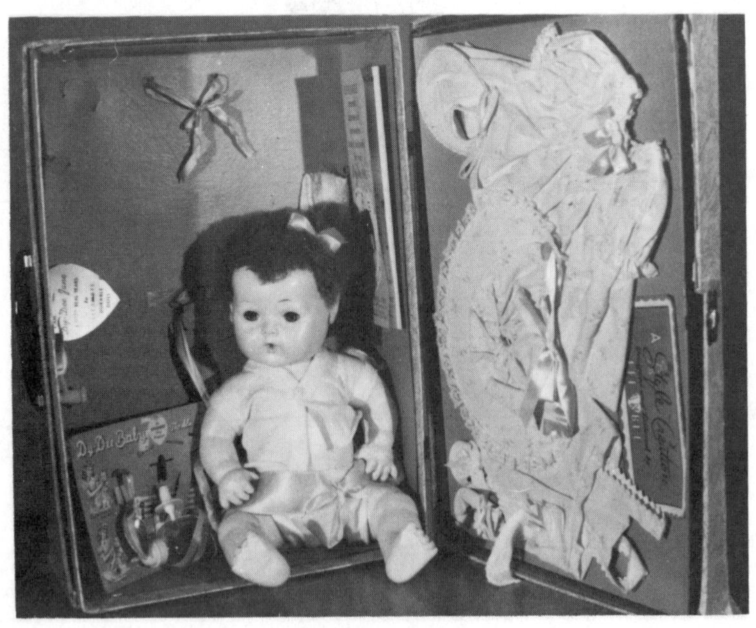

"Dy-Dee Jane"
16"
Original box
(H&J Foulke)

E.D. Bébé

MAKER: Unknown as yet but possibly by E. Denamur of Paris, France
DATE: Ca. 1885 into 1890's
MATERIAL: Bisque head, papier-mâché jointed body
SIZE: Various
MARK: "E D", and sometimes a size number

Marked E.D. BÉBÉ: Bisque head, papier-mâché jointed body, good wig, pierced ears, beautiful blown glass eyes, nicely dressed, good condition.

Closed Mouth	15-21"	$750-850
Open Mouth	15-20"	$425-500
	22-25"	$600-675

"E 9 D"
21" tall
New clothes
(H&J Foulke)

Eden Bébé

MAKER: Fleischmann & Bloedel of Fürth, Bavaria and Paris, France
DATE: Founded in Bavaria in 1873. Also in Paris by 1890, then on into S.F.B.J. in 1899
MATERIAL: Bisque head, papier-mâché body
SIZE: Various
MARK: "EDEN BÉBÉ, PARIS"

Marked Eden Bébé: Bisque head, jointed papier-mâché body with unjointed wrists, beautiful wig, large set paperweight eyes, pierced ears, lovely clothes, closed or open/closed mouth, all in nice condition.

Closed Mouth	10"	$400
	16"	$685-750
Open Mouth	18-20"	$400-450
	22-24"	$450-525
	27"	$600-650

"Eden Bebe Paris"
Walker
23" tall
(H&J Foulke)

Joel Ellis
(Wooden Doll)

MAKER: Co-operative Manufacturing Co., Springfield, Vt., U.S.A.

DATE: 1873

MATERIAL: Composition head, fully jointed wooden body. Metal feet and wooden or metal hands.

SIZE: 12" to 18"

MARK: None - unless black paper band around waist still exists with patent date printed on it.

Joel Ellis Wooden Doll: Composition head (over wood). Painted brown eyes, jointed wooden body (mortise-and-tenon), molded hair, metal hands and feet. Nicely dressed in old clothes. All in only fair condition.

Size 12" $450-550

Joel Ellis
12" tall
(Bertha Neumyer)

F.G. Bébé

MAKER: F. Gaultier, Paris (1860); later Gaultier and Fils, St. Maurice, Charenton, Seine, Paris, France
DATE: 1879 to 1900 and probably later
MATERIAL: Bisque head, jointed papier-mâché body
SIZE: Various
MARK: "F.G." or "F.G." in a scroll

Marked F.G. Bébé: Bisque head, papier-mâché body, good French wig, closed mouth, beautiful large set eyes, pierced ears, well dressed; all in nice condition.

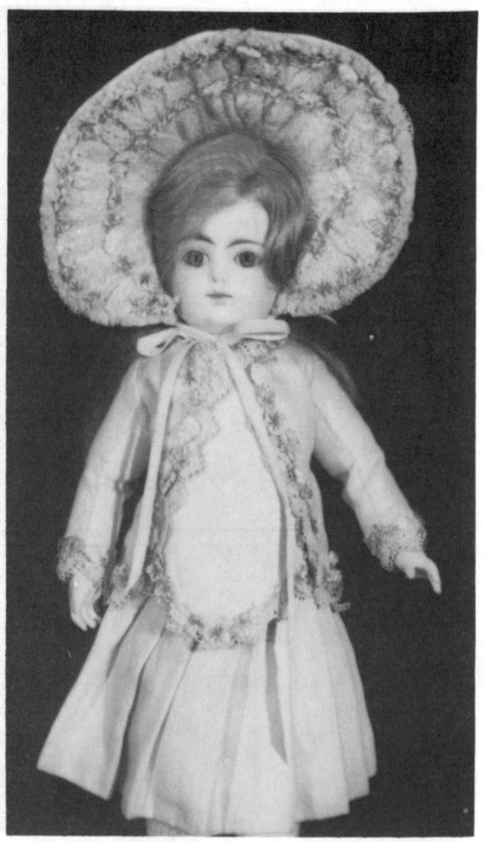

14-16" $700-800
20-24" $850-1,000

F.G. Bébé
14" tall
(Mike White)

F.G. Fashion

MAKER: Gaultier, A., Paris, (1860) later F. Gaultier and Fils, St. Maurice, Charenton, Seine and Paris, France
DATE: Late 1860's - on
MATERIAL: Bisque head, kid body
SIZE: Various
MARK: "F. G." on shoulder or head also size number

F. 8 G

Marked F. G. French Fashion: Bisque swivel head on bisque shoulder plate, original kid body, kid arms with wired fingers or bisque lower arms and hands; original or good French wig, lovely large stationary eyes, closed mouth, ears pierced; dressed; all in good condition.

11-12"	$450-500
16-19"	$575-675
24-25"	$900-950

"F. G."
15"
(Joyce Alderson)

F.G. - Gesland

MAKER: Heads: A. Gaultier, Paris; later F. Gaultier and Fils
Bodies: E., F. & A. Gesland, Paris
DATE: Late 1860's on
MATERIAL: Bisque head, stockinette stuffed body on wire frame. Bisque or composition lower arms and legs.
SIZE: Various
MARK: Heads - "F.G." or

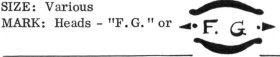

Gesland Bodied Dolls: Fashion lady bisque swivel head, pierced ears, closed mouth, paperweight eyes, good wig. Stockinette body with bisque lower arms and legs. Dressed. All in good condition. Size 16-23" $1,600-2,100

Bébé-type bisque swivel head, pierced ears, closed mouth, paperweight eyes, good wig. Stockinette body with composition lower arms and legs. Dressed. All in good condition. Size 20" $1,000 up*

*Not enough price samples to justify a reliable range.

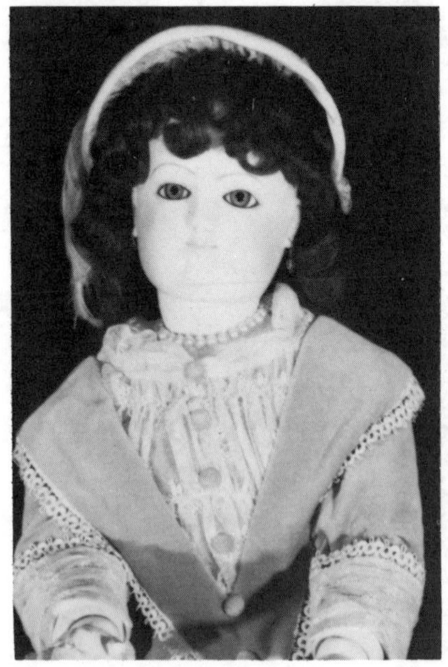

Rare Early Young Lady Type
F.G. on shoulder plate
Gesland stamp on body
Original advertising sheet in head
28" tall
(Mrs. H. Lewin)

Famlee Doll

MAKER: Berwick Doll Co. and Change-O-Doll Co., New York, N.Y., U.S.A.
DATE: 1918 - on
MATERIAL: Composition heads to screw onto cloth body, composition arms and legs
SIZE: 16"
MARK: PAT APR 12, 21 on screw cap

Famlee Doll: Three composition heads and one cloth body with threaded metal socket in top of body. Three sets of clothing. All in good condition. Size 16" $125

*Came in sets of up to 12 heads, so allow extra for each additional head.

Famlee Doll
with two extra heads
16" tall
Original clothes
(Bertha Neumyer)

Florodora

MAKER: Armand Marseille of Köppelsdorf, Thüringia, Germany
DATE: 1901
MATERIAL: Bisque head, composition ball-jointed body or kid jointed body
SIZE: Various
MARK:

Made in Germany
Florodora
A 2 M

Marked Florodora: Bisque head, composition ball-jointed or kid body, open mouth, sleep eyes, good wig, well dressed, all in good condition. Size 13-15" $100-125
Size 18-22" $150-165

Kid Body
"Florodora"
16" tall
(Emily Manning)

French Bébé

(Unmarked)

MAKER: Numerous French firms
DATE: Ca. 1860 to ca. 1925
MATERIAL: Bisque head, jointed papier-mâché body
SIZE: Various
MARK: None except perhaps numbers, Paris, or France

Unmarked French BÉBÉ: Beautiful bisque head, swivel neck, set paperweight eyes, ears pierced, closed mouth, lovely wig, jointed French body, pretty costume, all in good condition. Size 17-18" $700-750

Same as above except with open mouth. Size 16-22" $350-450

13

Open Mouth Walker
23" tall
(Joyce Alderson)

Closed Mouth
Kid body, 14" tall
(Joyce Alderson)

French Fashion-Unmarked

MAKER: Various French firms
DATE: Ca. 1860 through 1890's
MATERIAL: Bisque shoulder head; jointed kid body
SIZE: Various
MARK: None, except possibly numbers or letters

French Fashion: Unmarked bisque shoulder head, swivel neck, kid body, kid arms--some with wired fingers, or old bisque arms; original or good wig; lovely blown glass eyes, closed mouth, earrings, original or other fine clothes, all in very good condition.

11-13" $450-500
15-17" $575-700

Unmarked French Fashion
12" tall
(H & J Foulke)

French Fashion

(Wood Body)

MAKER: Unknown
DATE: Ca. 1865 - on
MATERIAL: Bisque head, fully jointed wood body
SIZE: Various
MARK: Size numbers only

Wood Body Lady: Bisque swivel head on shoulder plate, paperweight eyes, closed mouth, pierced ears, good wig. Wood body, fully jointed at shoulders, elbows, wrists, hips and knees. Dressed. All in good condition. 16-18" $1,100 up

*Rare with ball joint at waist and ankle joints.

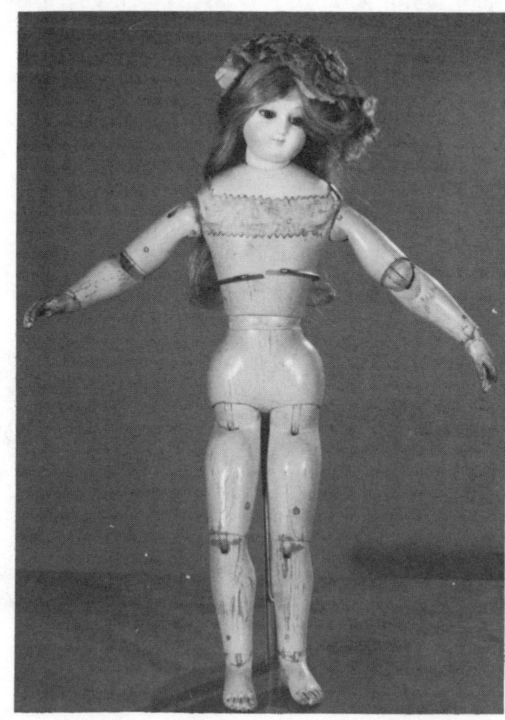

17" Wood Body
French Fashion
(Helen Teske)

Frozen Charlotte

MAKER: Various German firms
DATE: Ca. 1850's thru early 1900's
MATERIAL: Glazed china
SIZE: Various
MARK: None, except for "Germany", or numbers or both

Frozen Charlotte: All-china doll, black sometimes blond molded hair parted down the middle, painted features. Hands extended, legs separated but not jointed. No clothes; perfect condition.

2-4"	$25-50*
6"	$65*
13-15"	$300-350

*Allow extra for pink tone.

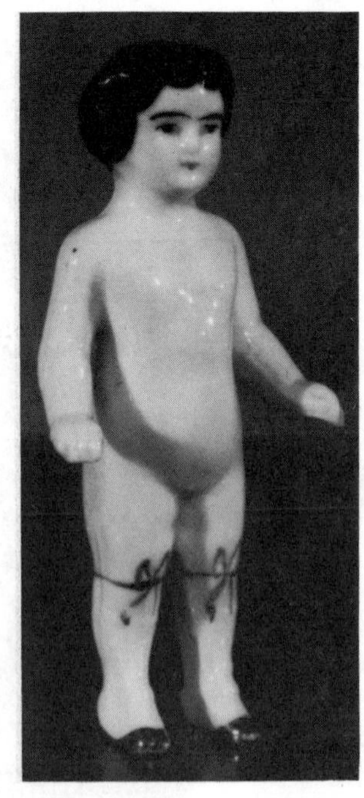

Frozen Charlotte
"200"
5" tall
Gold boots, blue garters
(H & J Foulke)

Fulper Dolls

MAKER: Fulper Pottery Co. of Flemington, N. J., U.S.A.
DATE: 1918 to 1921
MATERIAL: Bisque heads only by Fulper; used on bodies made by others
SIZE: Various
MARK: "Fulper -- Made in U.S.A." and others
Mark reproduced below.

Fulper Child Doll: Marked bisque head, good wig; kid jointed or composition ball-jointed body; set or sleep eyes, open mouth; suitably dressed. All in nice condition.
20-23" $250-300

Fulper Baby or Toddler: Same as above, but with bent-limb or jointed toddler body. 15-18" $200-300

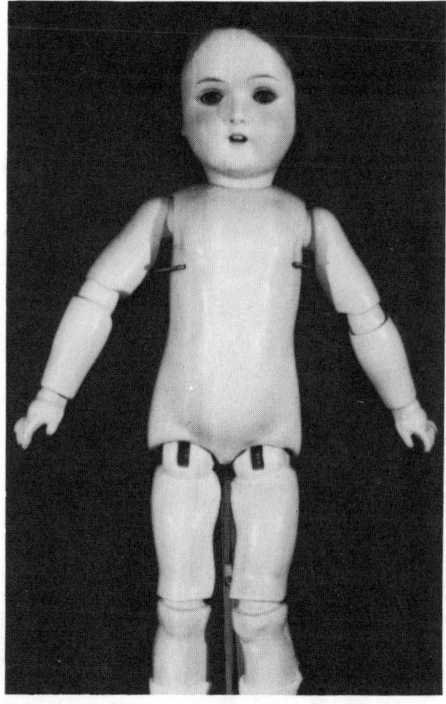

Marked "Fulper" head and "Victory Doll" body
Tin sleep eyes
23" tall
(H & J Foulke)

G.K. Child Doll

MAKER: Gebrüder Knoch of Neustadt near Coburg, Thüringia, Germany

DATE: Ca. 1908

MATERIAL: Bisque heads, composition stick-type jointed bodies

SIZE: Various

MARK: "Made in Germany"; numbers, such as 201, 199, 192

DEP

GK N — Made in Germany 201. 6/0 DEP.

Marked Knoch Child Doll: Bisque head, mohair wig, open mouth, sleep eyes; dressed; composition and wood stick-type body. Good condition. Size 12-14" $90-110

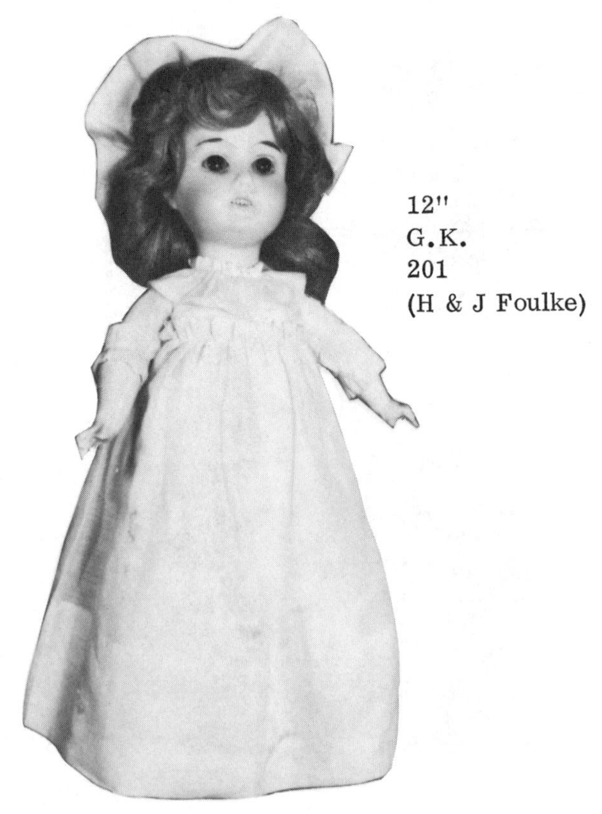

12"
G.K.
201
(H & J Foulke)

German Bisque Character Baby
(Unmarked)

MAKER: Various German firms
DATE: 1910 - on
MATERIAL: Bisque head, composition bent-limb body
SIZE: Various
MARK: Some numbered, some "Germany", some both

Unmarked Character Baby: Bisque head, good wig; or solid dome with painted hair, sleep eyes, open mouth; composition bent-limb baby body; suitably dressed; all in good condition.

7-9" $100-125
12-15" $150-185

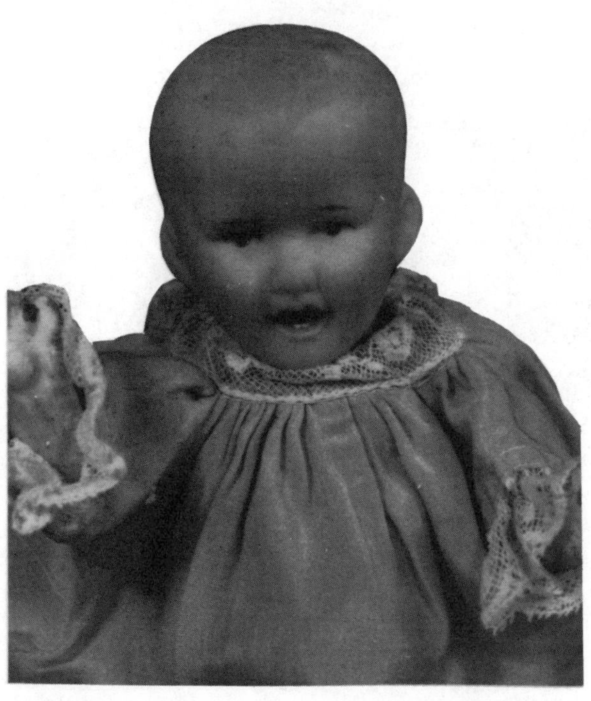

"Germany 243"; 7" tall (H&J Foulke)

German Bisque Child

(Open-mouth, Unmarked)

MAKER: Various German firms
DATE: Late 1880's to ca. 1940
MATERIAL: Bisque socket head, composition ball-jointed body; bisque shoulder head, kid body, bisque lower arms
SIZE: Various
MARK: Some with numbers and/or "Germany"

Unmarked Socket Head: Bisque head, ball-jointed composition body; good wig, open mouth, glass eyes, pretty clothes; all in nice condition.

13-16" $85-150*
20-23" $135-200*
25-28" $175-300*

Unmarked Shoulder Head: Bisque head, open mouth, glass eyes, good wig; kid or cloth body, bisque lower arms; dressed; all in good condition. Prices as above

*Higher price is for doll of exceptional quality.

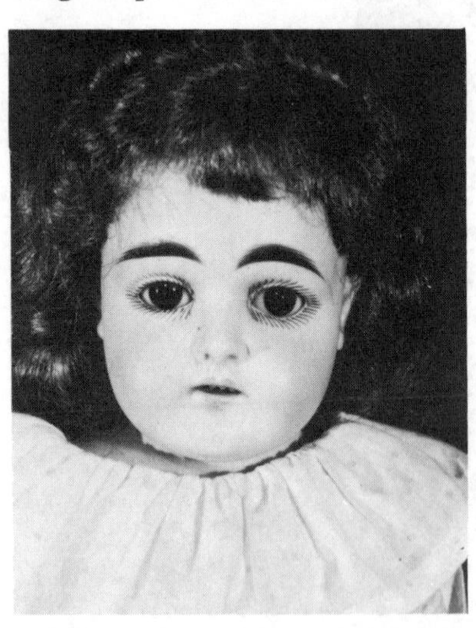

Left: German Bisque Shoulder Head/"27/118/Germany"; 20" tall (H&J Foulke)
Right: German Bisque Socket Head; composition body, 17" tall (H&J Foulke)

German Bisque Head
(Closed mouth, Unmarked)

MAKER: Various German firms
DATE: Ca. 1880 to ca. 1890
MATERIAL: Bisque shoulder heads; kid or cloth bodies, bisque hands. Bisque socket head; composition ball-jointed body
SIZE: Various
MARK: None except numbers

Unmarked Closed Mouth Doll: Bisque shoulder head, kid or cloth body, stitch jointed at shoulders, hips and knees; good bisque hands, nicely dressed; mohair wig; all in good condition.

16-18" $400-450*
22-25" $500-600*
Bisque socket head on composition body
15-18" $350-450
20-22" $475-500
25-28" $600-700

*Allow extra for swivel neck.

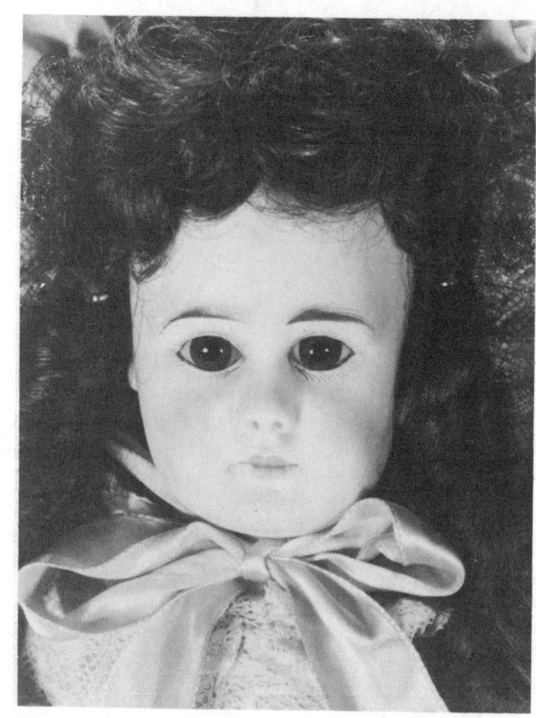

Unmarked Bisque Shoulder head
Bald head
16" tall
(H&J Foulke)

German Bisque Tiny Doll

MAKER: Various German firms
DATE: Ca. 1900 - on
MATERIAL: Bisque head, composition body
SIZE: Up to 12 inches
MARK: None except numbers, "Germany" or both

Tiny Child Doll: Bisque socket head, composition five-piece body, good wig, open mouth, set or sleep eyes, cute clothes; all in nice condition.

5-7" $45-65*
8-11" $60-125*

*Higher price is for body jointed at knees and elbows

Fully jointed body
9-1/2" tall
(H&J Foulke)

German Character Child
(Unmarked)

MAKER: Various German firms
DATE: 1910 - on
MATERIAL: Bisque head, jointed composition body
SIZE: Various
MARK: Numbers and "Germany"

Unmarked Character Child: Bisque head, character face with good wig or solid dome head with painted hair, sleep or painted eyes, open or closed mouth; jointed composition body; dressed; all in good condition.

Size 15-18" $350 up*
*Depending upon individual doll.

"183"
15" tall
(Clendenien Collection)

Ginny

MAKER: Vogue Dolls, Inc.
DATE: 1948 - on
MATERIAL: First, all composition; later - hard plastic
SIZE: 7" - 8"
CREATOR: Jennie Graves
CLOTHES DESIGNER: Virginia Graves Carlson
MARK: "Ginny/Vogue Dolls" - hard plastic; "Vogue" - composition

---

Composition Ginny: All composition, jointed neck, shoulders and hips; painted eyes looking to side, mohair wig. Original clothes. All in good condition. 7-8" $20

Hard plastic Ginny: All hard plastic, jointed at neck, shoulders and hips (some have jointed knees and some walk); sleep eyes (sometimes with molded lashes), nice wig. Original clothes. All in good condition. 7-8" $15 and up

8" tall
Ginny bent-knee walker
with wrist tag
All original
(Barbara Crescenze)

Gladdie

MAKER: Made in Germany for George Borgfeldt, New York, N.Y., U.S.A.

DATE: 1929

MATERIAL: Ceramic head, cloth torso, composition arms and legs

SIZE: 17" - 22"

DESIGNER: Helen W. Jensen

MARK: "Gladdie Copyriht [sic] Helen W. Jensen
Germany"

Marked Gladdie: Ceramic head, molded and painted hair, glass eyes, open-closed mouth with molded teeth, laughing face, cloth torso, composition arms and legs; dressed; all in good condition. Size 17" $500-600

Rare bisque head $1,200*

*Not enough price samples to justify a reliable range.

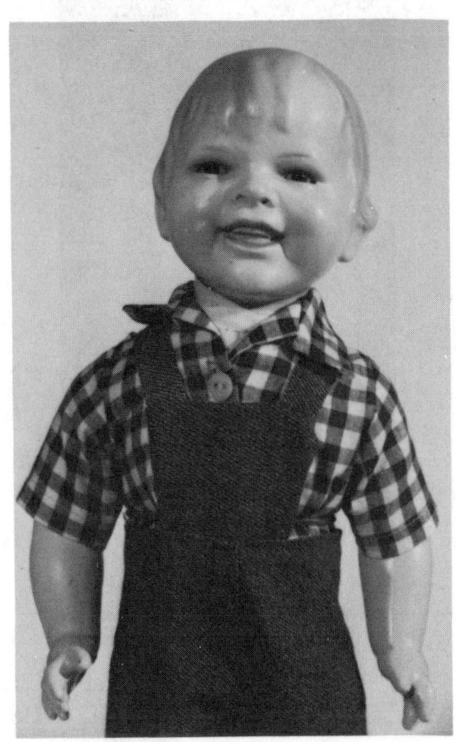

Gladdie
18" tall
(Clendenien Collection)

Goebel Dolls

MAKER: William Goebel, Thüringia, Germany
DATE: Ca. 1900 - on
MATERIAL: Bisque heads, composition bodies; also all bisque
SIZE: Various
MARK:

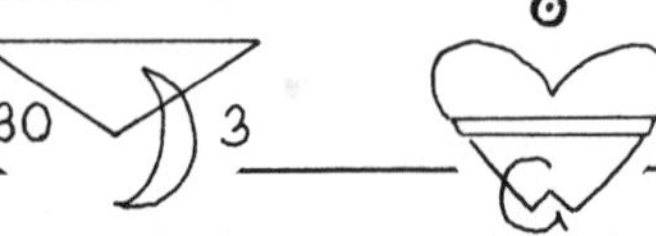

Goebel Child Doll: Bisque socket head, sleep eyes, open mouth, good wig, composition jointed body, dressed; in good condition. Size 23-25" $225-250

Goebel Character Doll: Bisque head with molded hair and painted features. Papier-Mâché body. Size 6-1/2" $250-275

Goebel Character Baby. Size 19-24" $325-385

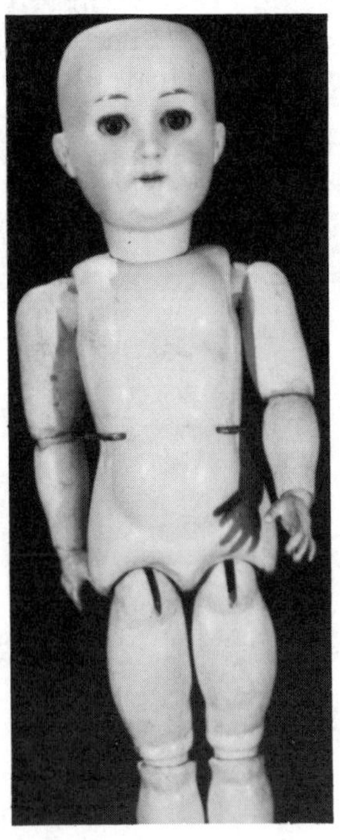

Left: 6-1/2" Goebel Character, (H & J Foulke)
Right: 21" Goebel Child (Emily Manning)

Googly-Eyed Doll

(All Bisque)

MAKER: J.D. Kestner and other German firms
DATE: Between WWI and WWII
MATERIAL: All bisque
SIZE: Usually under 6"
MARK: Various

All-bisque Googly: Jointed at shoulders and hips, molded shoes and socks, glass eyes, impish mouth, mohair wig. Undressed. In perfect condition. Size 4-5" $300-400*

Same as above, but with painted eyes. Size 4-5" $275-375*

*Allow extra for jointed neck and/or knees and elbows.

All bisque Kestner googly, 5" tall
Swivel neck
Jointed at shoulders, elbows, hips and knees
(Betty Harms)

Googly-Eyed Dolls
(Glass Eyes)

MAKER: Armand Marseille, J.D. Kestner, other German and French firms
DATE: Between World War I and World War II
MATERIAL: Bisque head, composition body
SIZE: Various
MARK: Various

Googly-eyed Doll: Marked bisque head; original composition body jointed at neck, shoulders and hips; molded and painted socks and shoes, googly eyes look to side, sleep or set; impish mouth closed, proper wig, cute clothes; all in nice condition.

Usually A.M. #323 or 253 7-8" $425-475
9" $550-600
J.D.K. #221 14" $2,000 up

AM 323
7" tall
(H&J Foulke)

Googly-Eyed Doll
(Painted Eyes)

MAKER: Armand Marseille and other German firms
DATE: Between World War I and II
MATERIAL: Bisque head, composition body
SIZE: Usually under 10 inches
MARK: Various

Painted-Eye Googly: Marked bisque swivel head with painted eyes to side, molded hair, impish mouth; composition body jointed at shoulders and hips with molded and painted shoes and socks. Cute clothes. All in good condition.

Size 7-8" $235-275

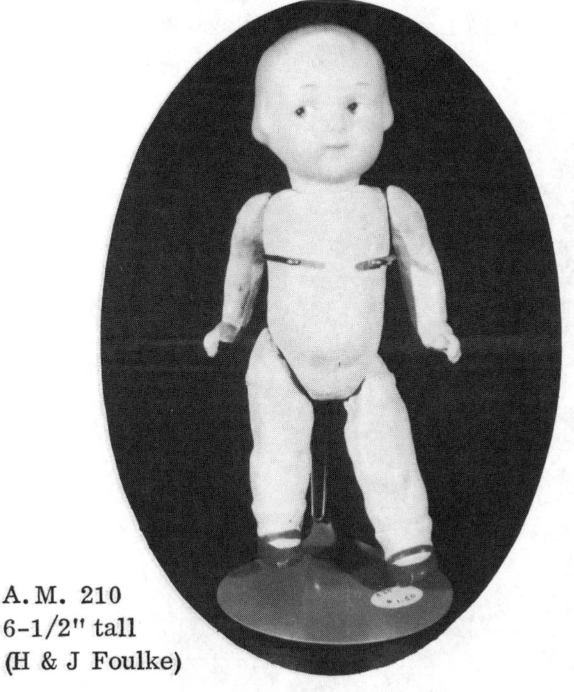

A.M. 210
6-1/2" tall
(H & J Foulke)

Greiner

MAKER: Ludwig Greiner of Philadelphia, Penn., U.S.A.
DATE: 1858 to 1883
MATERIAL: Heads of papier-mâché; cloth bodies, homemade in most cases, but later some Lacmann bodies were used.
SIZE: Various, 13" to over 35"
MARK: Paper label on back shoulder:

GREINER'S
IMPROVED
PATENTHEADS
Pat. March 30TH '58

GREINER'S
PATENT DOLL HEADS
No 7
Pat. Mar. 30 '58. Ext. '72

Greiner: Blond or black molded hair, painted features; complete late label, homemade cloth body, leather arms, nice old clothes; entire doll in nice condition.

1872 Label:	20-21"	\$200-225
	25"	\$250
1858 Label:	21-23"	\$225-250
	26-28"	\$275-300

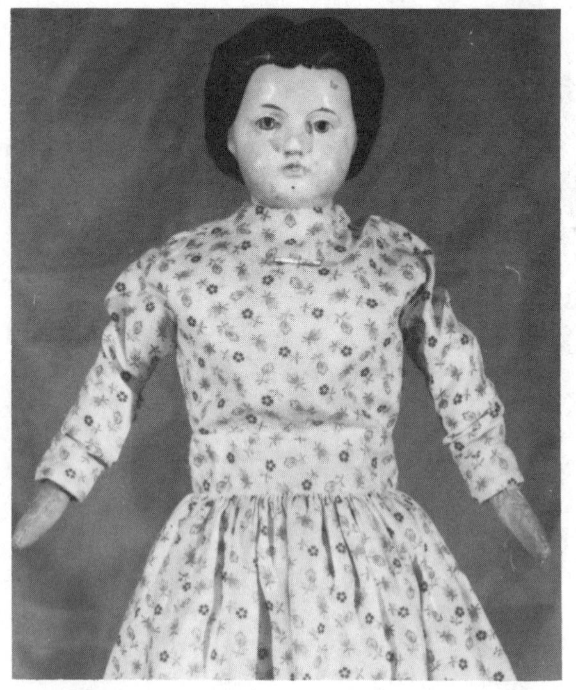

"Greiners Pat. Doll Heads/Pat. Mar. 30 '58. Ext '72"
20" tall
(H & J Foulke)

Half-Bisque Dolls

MAKER: Unknown
DATE: 1910
MATERIAL: Bisque with cloth upper legs and arms
SIZE: 4-1/2" - 6-1/2"
MARK: "Germany"

Half-Bisque Dolls: Head and body to waist of one-piece bisque, molded hair, painted features, bisque hands, lower legs with white stockings and molded shoes with heels and bows, other parts of body are cloth. Appropriate clothes. All in good condition.

Size 6-1/2" $100-110

For photo see, ALL-BISQUE & HALF-BISQUE DOLLS, Angione, p. 40, illustration # 3.

Heinrich Handwerck Child Doll

MAKER: Heinrich Handwerck of Waltershausen, Thüringia, Germany

DATE: Ca. 1890 - on

MATERIAL: Bisque head, composition ball-jointed body

SIZE: Various

MARK: "Germany - Handwerck" sometimes with "S & H" and numbers, such as 109, 119 etc.

Hch 6/0 H.
Germany

Marked Handwerck Child Doll: Bisque socket head, ball-jointed body, open mouth, sleep or set eyes, original or good wig, pierced ears, lovely old clothes; entire doll in good condition.

16-19"	$150-195
23-26"	$225-250
27-30"	$275-325
31-33"	$350-400
34-36"	$400+

"109
Germany"
17" tall
All original
(H & J Foulke)

Max Handwerck Child Doll

MAKER: Max Handwerck of Waltershausen, Thüringia, Germany
DATE: 1900 - on
MATERIAL: Bisque socket head, ball-jointed composition body
SIZE: Various
MARK: "Max Handwerck" numbers and sometimes "Germany"; also Bébé Elite

---

Marked Max Handwerck Child Doll: Marked bisque socket head; original or good wig, original ball-jointed body, pierced ears, set or sleep eyes, open mouth; well dressed; all in good condition.

22-25" $200-225
Bébé Elite Character:
16" $210-225

"Max Handwerck
288 - 28.5
Germany"
20" tall
All original
(H & J Foulke)

Hansi & Gresel

MAKER: P.J. Gallais & Co., Paris, France
DATE: 1921 - 1925
MATERIAL: Earthenware
SIZE: 7-1/2 inches
MARK: None on doll; paper wrist tag "Vive la France! Gresel" on the other side "Hansi"

Hansi or Gresel: Earthenware head with painted eyes and hair, closed mouth; jointed five-piece earthenware body with painted shoes and socks; original clothes. All in good condition.

Size 7-1/2" $175-200

"Gresel"
7-1/2" tall
All original
(Becky Roberts)

Happifats

MAKER: Registered by Borgfeldt in U.S. and Germany
DATE: 1913 - 1921
MATERIAL: All composition or all bisque or composition head and hands with stuffed body
SIZE: All bisque 3-1/2" - 4-1/2"; composition - about 10"
DESIGNER: Kate Jordan
MARK: ©

Happifats: All bisque with jointed arms, painted features, molded clothes.

3-1/2 to 4-1/2" $150 (German)
3-1/2 to 4-1/2" $100 (Japanese)
Composition $100*
*Not enough price samples to justify a reliable range.

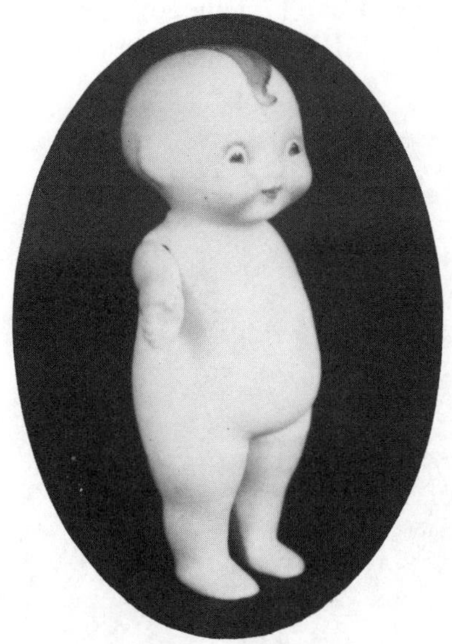

Happifat Baby
3-1/2"
(H & J Foulke)

HEbee-SHEbee Dolls

MAKER: Edward Imeson Horsman Co., New York, N.Y., (EIH), U.S.A. (All bisques made in Germany)
DATE: 1925
MATERIAL: Composition; some all bisque
SIZE: Various
DESIGNER: Charles H. Twelvetrees
MARK: Sticker on foot

HEbee-SHEbee Doll: All-composition, jointed at shoulders and hips. Painted eyes; molded white chemise and real ties in molded shoes. Gummed label on foot. All in fair condition. 10-1/2" Tall. $175-225

All bisque, jointed at shoulders and hips. Molded white chemise, real ties in molded shoes (German). Size 4-5" $400 up

All bisque with molded cap (Japanese). Size 4-5" $100 up

Blue shoes indicate a "HEbee"; pink ones a "SHEbee".

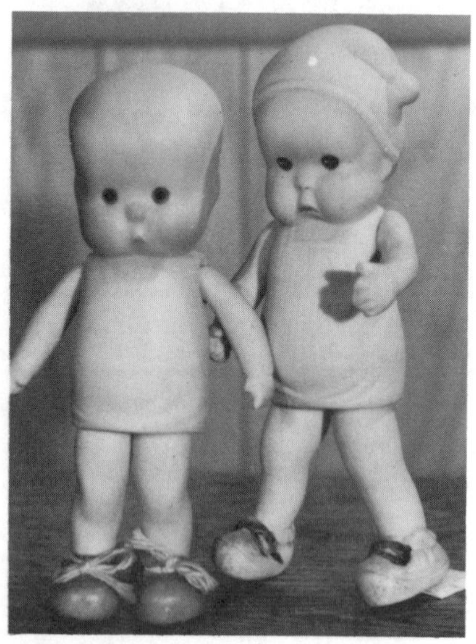

Left: HEbee, 5-1/2" tall (German)
Right: HEbee with rare molded cap, "Made in Japan", both dolls from the collection of Bertha Neumyer.

Sonja Henie
(Mme. Alexander)

MAKER: Alexander Doll Co., Inc., New York, N.Y., U.S.A.
DATE: 1939
MATERIAL: Composition, jointed at neck, shoulders and hips
SIZE: 14", 18", 21"
MARK: "Madame Alexander -- Sonja Henie" embossed on back of neck or on shoulders

---

Marked Sonja Henie: All composition, jointed as above; smiling open mouth with teeth, sleep eyes, lovely human hair wig, original clothes and shoe skates; all in very nice condition.

Size 17-18" $125-150

Sonja Henie
14" tall
Original skates and button
New dress
(Rosemary Dent)

Gebrüder Heubach

MAKER: Gebrüder Heubach of Licht and Sonneberg, Thüringia, Germany
DATE: Dolls considered here mostly from 1910 - on
MATERIAL: Bisque head, kid or cloth or jointed composition body or composition bent-limb body
SIZE: Various
MARK: "Gebrüder Heubach - Germany"

Heubach Character Doll: Marked bisque head, character face, molded hair, intaglio eyes; jointed composition or kid body closed or open/closed mouth, dressed; all in nice condition. 12-16" $350 and up depending upon character

Heubach Infants: Marked bisque head, molded hair or good wig, character face, composition bent-limb body; open or closed mouth, sleep or intaglio eyes, dressed; all in nice condition. 8-10" $200-225

Left: Coquette, 11" tall, compo body(Clendenien Col.), $425-450
Right: Pouty girl, 16" tall, compo body(Richard Wright) $600 up

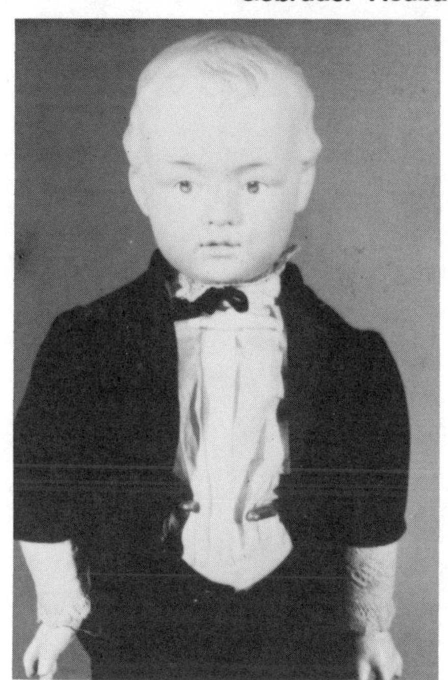

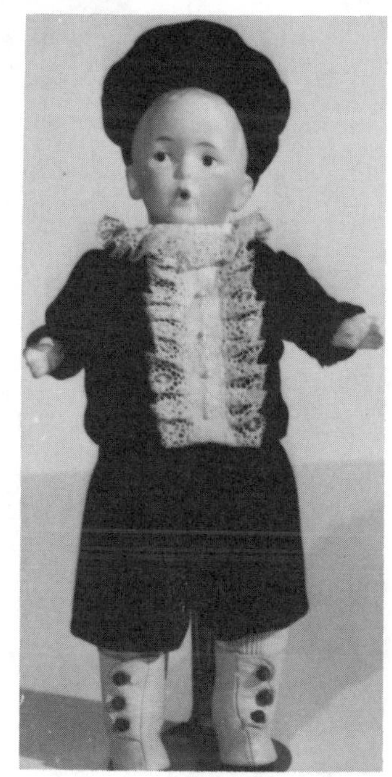

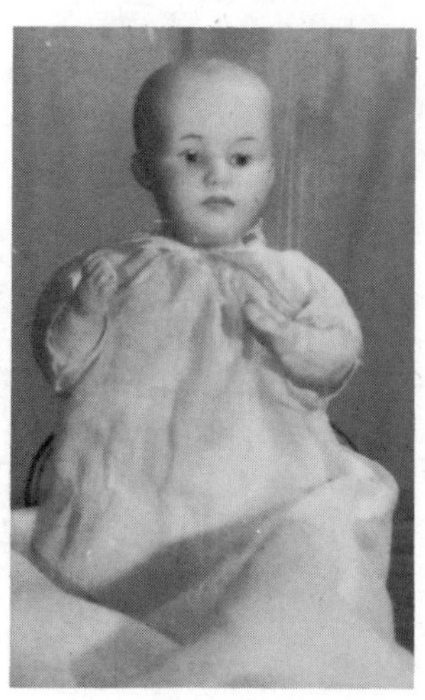

Left Top: Character boy, 17" tall, composition body (Helen Teske) $550

Right Top: Whistling Jim, 11" tall, hole in mouth (Clendenien Collection) $700

Right Bottom: Infant, 6" tall, 5-piece baby body (Bertha Neumyer) $150-175

Left: The Winker, 9-1/2" tall, 5-piece toddler body (Richard Wright) $400

Right: Child # 8192 17" tall, composition body (H & J Foulke) $225-250

Heubach Köppelsdorf Character Baby

MAKER: Ernst Heubach of Köppelsdorf, Thüringia, Germany
DATE: 1910 - on
MATERIAL: Bisque socket head, composition bent-limb baby or toddler body
SIZE: 8 - 25"
MARK: "Heubach Köppelsdorf, Germany" and numbers, often 300, 320, 342

Marked Heubach Character Baby: Bisque socket head, good wig, sleep eyes, open mouth (wobbly tongue, pierced nostrils sometimes); composition bent-limb or toddler body; dressed; in good condition.

14-18" $200-250
22-25" $275-325

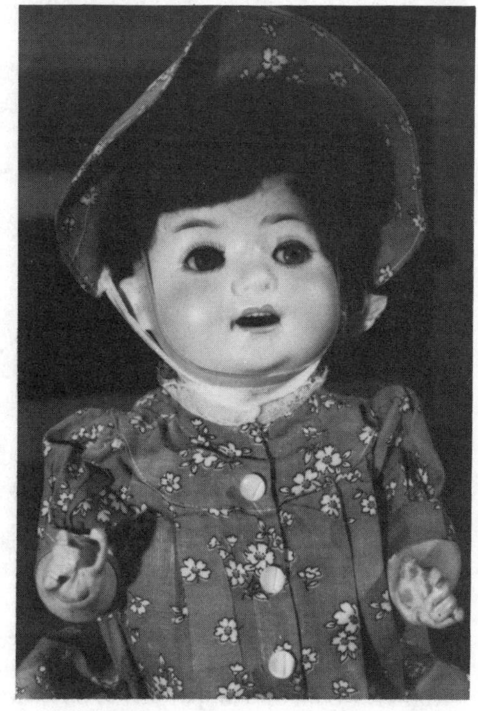

"Heubach Köppelsdorf
300/0
Germany"
15-1/2" tall
(H & J Foulke)

Heubach Köppelsdorf Child Doll

MAKER: Ernst Heubach of Köppelsdorf, Thüringia, Germany
DATE: 1887 - well into the 20th century
MATERIAL: Bisque head, jointed kid or jointed composition bodies
SIZE: Various
MARK: "Heubach Köppelsdorf, Germany" and sometimes horseshoe mark; numbers, often 275 (shoulder head) and 250 (socket head)

Heubach Girl Doll: Marked bisque head, good wig, sleep eyes, open mouth, jointed composition body, cute clothes; all in nice condition. 16-20" $125-150, 29-33" $265-295

Heubach Shoulder Head: Marked bisque head, kid or cloth body, bisque arms, sleep or set eyes, open mouth, good wig, dressed; all in nice condition. 20-23" $135-165

Left: "Heubach Köppelsdorf/250/Germany", 5-piece composition body, 9" tall, all original (H & J Foulke)

Right: "Heubach Köppelsdorf/250/Germany", 24" tall, original clothes (H & J Foulke)

Heubach Köppelsdorf Gypsy & Black Baby

MAKER: Ernst Heubach of Köppelsdorf, Thüringia, Germany
DATE: Ca. late 1920's
MATERIAL: Bisque head, bent-limb composition or toddler body with composition arms and legs
SIZE: Various
MARK: "Heubach Köppelsdorf 399 - 16/0 Germany - D.R.G.M." on black baby; "Heubach Koppelsdorf 452 10/0 Germany" on gypsy

---

Heubach Köppelsdorf Black Baby: Marked black bisque head, bent-limb or toddler black body, closed mouth, molded hair or black kinky wig, original grass skirt and brass jewelry, sleep eyes; all in fine condition. Size 7-10" $225 -325

Heubach Köppelsdorf Gypsy: Marked tan bisque head, matching toddler body, open mouth with teeth, mohair wig, brass earrings, sleeping eyes. Appropriate costume. All in good condition. Size 10-12" $200-225*

*Not enough price samples to justify a reliable range.

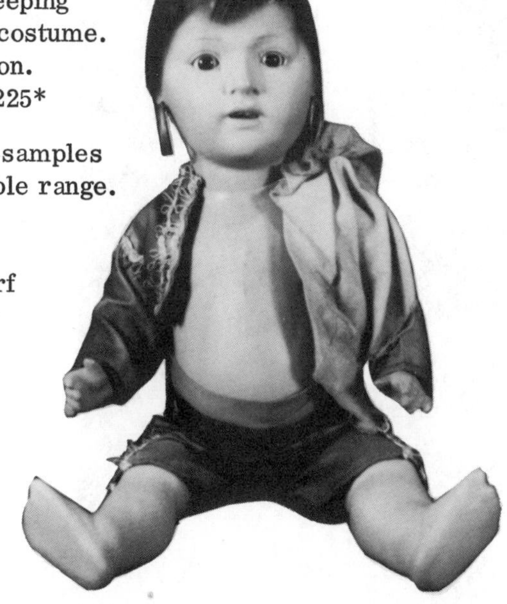

Gypsy
"Heubach Köppelsdorf
452 - 10/0
Germany"
12" tall
(Richard Wright)

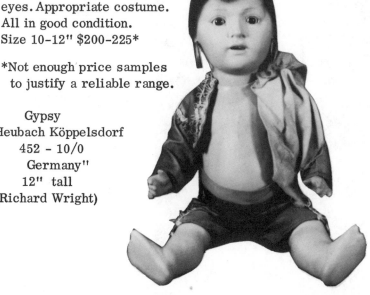

Hilda

MAKER: J.D. Kestner, Jr. of Waltershausen, Thüringia, Germany
DATE: 1914
MATERIAL: Bisque socket head, composition bent-limb baby body
SIZE: Various
MARK: "Made in Germany 245 JDK, Jr. 1914 © Hilda"; also sometimes 237; also 1070 on bald head variety

Hilda
©
J.D.K. Jr. 190
Gesgesch 1070
made in Germany

Kestner "Hilda": Marked bisque head, composition bent-limb baby body, sleep eyes, open mouth, dressed; all in good condition.

With wig:

14-16"	$750-800
20-23"	$900-1100

Bald:

14-16"	$750-800
20-24"	$1100-1200

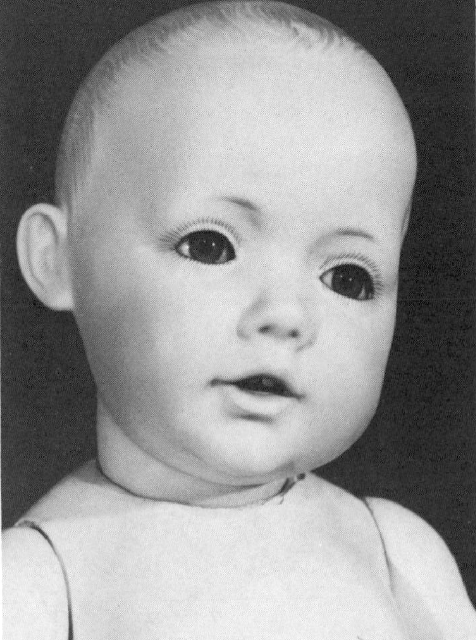

Hilda marked
"JDK
Ges gesch 12 K1070
Made in Germany"
16" tall
(H & J Foulke)

Historical Dolls

(Replicas)

MAKER: EFFanBEE Doll Co., New York, N.Y., U.S.A.
DATE: 1939
MATERIAL: All composition
SIZE: 14" - 15" depending on hairdo
MARK: "EFFanBEE Anne-Shirley" on body; metal EFFanBEE heart bracelet

---

Replica Historical Doll: All composition, painted features, hair wigs, excellent quality. Original costume. All in very good condition. Size 14-15" $125 up

Note: This was a series of 30 dolls portraying the history of American fashion 1565-1939. There were three sets of originals made, which were 20" tall with heads marked "American Children." These were all sold to private collectors.

"Settling of the West 1888"
14-15" tall
(Rosemary Dent)

Holz-Masse

(Composition Head)

MAKER: Cuno & Otto Dressel, Sonneburg, Thüringia, Germany
DATE: 1875 - on
MATERIAL: Composition head, arms and legs; cloth body
SIZE: Various
MARK:

Marked Holz-Masse: Composition shoulder head, mohair wig, glass or painted eyes, sometimes pierced ears. Cloth body with composition arms and legs with molded boots. Old clothes. All in good condition.

Size 18-21" $225-250

Holz - Masse
17"
All original
(Helen Teske)

Mary Hoyer

MAKER: The Mary Hoyer Doll Mfg. Co., Reading, Penn. U.S.A.
DATE: Ca. 1925 - 1950
MATERIAL: First all composition; later all hard plastic
SIZE: 14 inches
MARK: Embossed on torso "The/Mary Hoyer/Doll"
or
"ORIGINAL/Mary Hoyer/Doll"
(in a circle)

Marked Mary Hoyer: Material as above, swivel neck, jointed shoulders and hips. Sleep eyes with lashes, closed mouth, original wig. Appropriate old clothes (many are crocheted). All in good condition.

Composition 14" $45-55
Hard Plastic 14" $40-50

For photo see, MORE TWENTIETH CENTURY DOLLS, page 828, illustration HOY-3.

Hug Me Kiddies

MAKER: Unknown, but distributed by Samstag & Hilder, New York, N.Y., U.S.A.
DATE: 1912 - 1914
MATERIAL: Composition mask face, felt body
SIZE: 9-1/2" - 14"
MARK: None on doll; paper label on clothing

Hug Me Kiddies: Round composition mask face, round glass eyes looking to side, wig, watermelon mouth, felt body, original clothes; all in good condition. Size 14" $275-300

14" tall
Original clothes
(H & J Foulke)

A. Hülss

MAKER: Adolf Hülss of Walterhausen, Thüringia, Germany; heads by Simon & Halbig
DATE: 1915 - 1925
MATERIAL: Bisque socket heads, composition bodies (later heads of painted bisque)
SIZE: Various
MARK:

SIMON & HALBIG

AH
W
Made
in
Germany
156/32

Baby: 17-22" $275-325
Toddler, original costume:
10-11" $235-265

As above but 156/2
9-3/4" tall
All original
(H & J Foulke)

Hummel Dolls
(Rubber)

MAKER: Wm. Goebel, Porzellanfabrik, Germany
DATE: Circa 1940's
MATERIAL: All rubber
SIZE: 11-12"
DESIGNER: M.I. Hummel
MARK: Signed head, tagged clothes, also paper label

Hummel Doll: Rubber head, molded, painted hair, painted features; jointed neck, shoulders and hips. Original clothes. All in good condition. Size 12" $85-95*

*Hummel dolls are now being made in vinyl. Do not pay old prices for new dolls.

"Christl"
Original clothes and box
12" tall
(Jan Foulke)

Huret Fashion

MAKER: Maison Huret, Paris, France
DATE: 1850 - on
MATERIAL: Heads - china or bisque; bodies - gutta percha, kid, wood or papier-mâché
SIZE: Various
MARK: "Huret", "Maison Huret" stamped on body

HURET

Marked Huret: China or bisque shoulder head, closed mouth, painted or glass eyes, good wig, kid or wooden jointed body, beautifully dressed; all in good condition.

$1500 and up*

* More for portrait face.

Huret-type
Kid body
16" tall
(Joyce Alderson)

Indian Doll

(Bisque Head)

MAKER: Armand Marseille of Köppelsdorf, Thüringia, Germany and others
DATE: Ca. 1894 - on
MATERIAL: Bisque head, jointed composition body
SIZE: Various
MARK: "A.M." - sometimes "Germany"; many unmarked

Indian Doll: Bisque head, composition body, jointed shoulders and hips, entire doll light brown or "Indian copper color"; character face, worry wrinkles between brows, brown set glass eyes, black wig in braids, original clothes, head feathers, moccasins or molded shoes; all in good condition.

8-12"
$100-150
14-15"
$165-225

Indian Brave
and Maiden
All original
9"
(H&J Foulke)

J.V. Child Doll

MAKER: J. Verlingue of Boulogne-sur-Mer, France
DATE: 1914 to ca. 1919
MATERIAL: Bisque head, papier-mâché body
SIZE: Various
MARK: "PETITE FRANÇAISE --FRANCE"
Liane

PETITE FRANÇAISE
FRANCE
J V
3/0D
LIANE

Marked J.V. Child: Bisque head, jointed papier-mâché body; good wig, glass eyes, open mouth, nicely dressed.

Size 12-14" $175-225
Size 21-23" $300-375

All bisque w/swivel neck
Size 7" $175-200

"Petite Francaise"
16" tall
(Joyce Alderson)

Japanese Traditional Doll

MAKER: Various
DATE: 1850's - on
MATERIAL: Papier-mâché head, hips, arms and legs, cloth body
SIZE: Very small to very large
MARK: None

Traditional Japanese: Papier-mâché swivel head on shoulder plate, hips, lower legs and feet (early ones have jointed wrists and ankles). Cloth mid-section, cloth (floating) upper arms and legs. Pierced ears and nostrils. Hair wigs. Dark glass eyes, original or appropriate clothes; all in good condition.

<u>20th Century</u>:

12-14"	$25-35
22-24"	$50-75

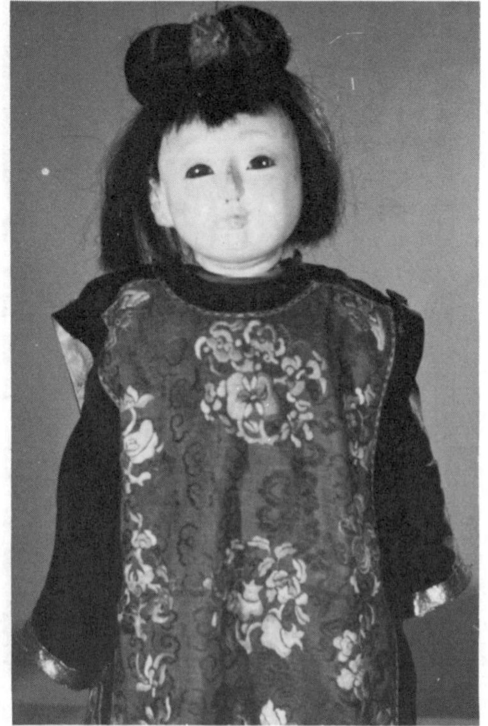

Traditional Japanese
24" tall
(Helen Teske)

Jullien Bébé

MAKER: Jullien, Jeune of Paris, France
DATE: 1875 to 1904 when they joined S.F.B.J.
MATERIAL: Bisque head, composition and wood body
SIZE: Various
MARK: "JULLIEN" with size number

JULLIEN
1

Marked Jullien Bébé: Bisque head, jointed wood and composition body; lovely wig, paperweight eyes, closed mouth, pierced ears, pretty old clothes, all in good condition.

20-24" $900-1100
Same as above with open mouth:
21-25" $500-600

Jullien
21" tall
(Richard Wright)

Jumeau

(Princess Elizabeth)

MAKER: S.F.B.J., Paris, France
DATE: 1938
MATERIAL: Bisque head, jointed, composition body
SIZE: Various
MARK:

UNIS FRANCE
71 149
306
JUMEAU
1938
PARIS

Late Jumeau: Bisque socket head highly colored, with glass flirty eyes and closed mouth, good wig. Jointed composition body. Dressed. All in good condition. Size 19" $400-425

Jumeau
15" tall
(Joyce Alderson)

Jumeau Bébé

(E.J.)

MAKER: Maison Jumeau, Paris, France (Emile Jumeau)
DATE: Ca. 1880
MATERIAL: Bisque socket head, composition body
SIZE: Various
MARK: Head - DÉPOSÉ E. 7 J. Body JUMEAU MEDAILLE D'OR PARIS

Marked (E.J.): Bisque socket head with closed mouth, paperweight eyes, pierced ears, good wig; jointed composition body with straight wrists; lovely clothes; all in good condition.

Size 14-17" $1250-1350
Size 19-23" $1400-1500

"Depose
E 12 J"
26" tall
All original
(Helen Teske)

Jumeau Bébé

(Long-face or Cody)

MAKER: Maison Jumeau, Paris, France
DATE: Ca. 1870's
MATERIAL: Bisque head, jointed papier-mâché body
SIZE: Various
MARK: Number only on head; "Jumeau Medaille D'or", on body

JUMEAU
MEDAILLE D'OR
PARIS

Long-face Jumeau: Bisque socket head with beautiful wig, closed mouth, applied pierced ears, blown glass eyes; jointed composition body with straight wrists; lovely clothes; all in good condition. Size 30-34" $3,500 up

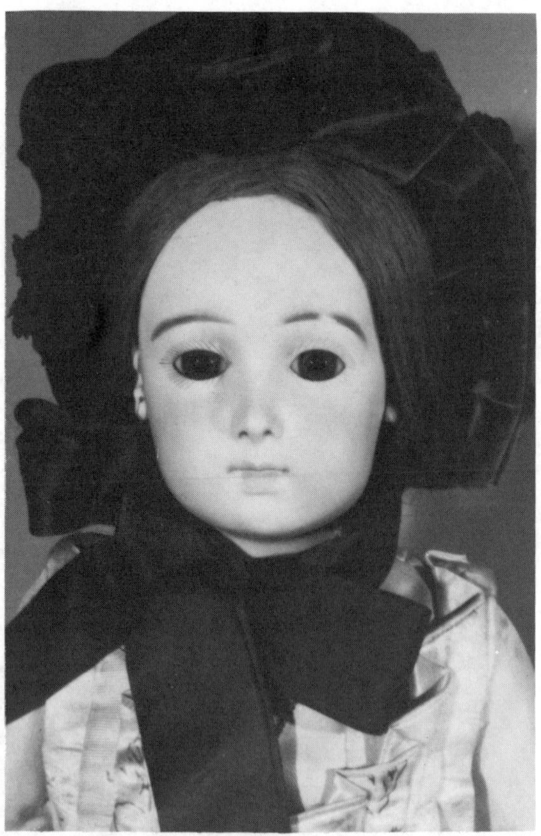

Long-face Jumeau
24" tall
(Helen Teske)

Jumeau Bébé

(So-called Portrait)

MAKER: Maison Jumeau, Paris, France
DATE: Ca. 1870's
MATERIAL: Bisque head, jointed composition body
SIZE: Various
MARK: Head - size only
Body - Sometimes "Jumeau Medaille D'or"

Portrait Jumeau: Bisque socket head with unusually large paperweight eyes, pierced ears, closed mouth, skin or other good wig; jointed composition body with straight wrists; nicely dressed. All in good condition. 16" $1,300-1,500

Left: 22" tall, blue stamp on body, all original (Richard Wright)
Right: 9", Size O, blue stamp on body (Mike White)

Jumeau Bébé

(Tête)

MAKER: Maison Jumeau, Paris, France
DATE: 1879 to 1899 - then through S.F.B.J.
MATERIAL: Bisque head, jointed papier-mâché body
SIZE: Various
MARK: "TÊTE JUMEAU" on head (red stamp)
Body - Jumeau stamp or "Bébé Jumeau" oval sticker

DÉPOSÉ
TETE JUMEAU
B^TE SGDG
6

Tête Jumeau: Bisque head, original or good French wig, beautiful stationary eyes, closed mouth, pierced ears, jointed composition body with jointed or straight wrists; original or lovely clothes; all in good condition.

9-10"	$1,000
12-14"	$900-1,000
17-22"	$1,000-1,100
24-27"	$1,250-1,400

Same as above but with open mouth, may be unmarked or incised 1907.

16-20"	$425-500
22-24"	$500-575
27-30"	$625-725

Tête Jumeau
Marked head & body
19" tall
(H & J Foulke)

Jumeau Fashion

MAKER: Maison Jumeau, Paris, France
DATE: Late 1860's - on
MATERIAL: Bisque head, kid body
SIZE: Various
MARK: Head - usually size only
Body - Blue stamped

JUMEAU
MEDAILLE D'OR
PARIS

Marked Jumeau Fashion: Bisque swivel head on shoulder plate, paperweight eyes, pierced ears, closed mouth, good wig. All kid body or kid with bisque lower arms and legs. Appropriate clothes. All in good condition. 16-19" $650-850
21-23" $900-1,000

Jumeau
Blue Body Stamp
Young lady-type
Fashion Doll
(Helen Teske)

Jumeau Phonograph Doll

MAKER: Maison Jumeau, Paris, France
DATE: 1890's
MATERIAL: Bisque head, composition body with a cavity in torso to accommodate a small phonograph.
SIZE: Usually 24-25"
MARK: Head - A regular Jumeau head with open mouth
Body - Blue stamp "Jumeau"

Jumeau Phonograph: Regular bisque Jumeau head with open mouth, paperweight eyes, pierced ears, good wig. Jointed composition body as above with Lioret phonograph and wax cylinder wound by key protruding from doll's back.

Size 24" $650-750*

*Not enough price samples to justify a reliable range.

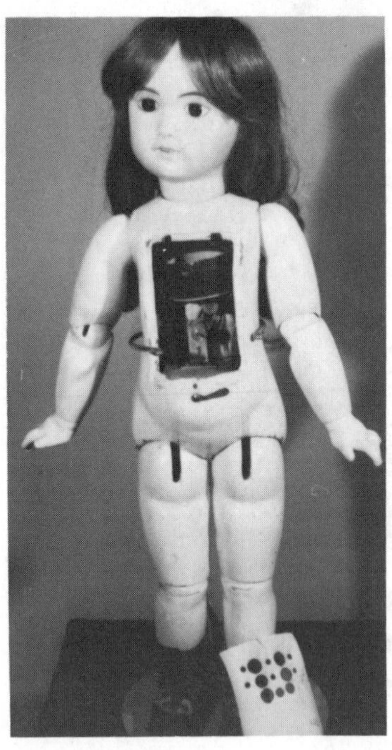

"Jumeau
230
Paris"
Phonograph body with blue Jumeau Medaille d'Or stamp
24" tall
(Helen Teske)

Just Me Doll

MAKER: Armand Marseille of Köppelsdorf, Thüringia, Germany
DATE: Ca. 1925
MATERIAL: Bisque socket head, composition jointed body
SIZE: Various small sizes
MARK: "Just Me A. M. 310 Germany"

Marked "Just Me": Bisque socket head, glass eyes to side, closed mouth, curly wig; composition body, dressed; all in good condition. Size 7-1/2" $500-600

Painted bisque socket head. Size 7-1/2" $150-175

"Just Me/A. M. 310/
Germany"
9-1/2" tall
Painted bisque head
5-piece compo body
All original
(H & J Foulke)

Jutta Dolls

MAKER: Cuno and Otto Dressel, Sonneberg, Thüringia, Germany. Heads by Simon & Halbig and others.
DATE: 1906 - 1921
MATERIAL: Bisque head, composition body
SIZE: Various
MARK: "Jutta S & H" also numbers 1348 and 1349 for girl dolls; 1914 for character baby

Jutta
1914
8

1349
Jutta
S & H
11

Marked S & H Jutta Girl: Bisque socket head, open mouth, sleep eyes, pierced ears, good wig; ball-jointed composition body; dressed; all in good condition.

Size: 19-20" $225 - 250

Marked Jutta Character Baby: Bisque socket head, open mouth, sleep eyes, good wig; bent-limb composition baby body; dressed; all in good condition.

Size: 22-23" $250 - 295

Left: "Jutta 1349 S&H"
17" tall (H&J Foulke)
Right: "Jutta 1914"
14" tall (Emily Manning)

K & R Character

MAKER: Kämmer & Reinhardt of Waltershausen, Thüringia, Germany
DATE: 1910 - on
MATERIAL: Bisque socket head, composition ball-jointed body
SIZE: Various
MARK: "K(star)R", sometimes with "S & H", often "Germany". Numbers, such as 101, 107, 109, 114, 117, 116A

K (star with &) R
SIMON & HALBIG
116/A

Marked K(star)R Character Doll: Bisque socket head, good wig, painted or glass eyes, closed mouth, composition ball-jointed body, nicely dressed; all in good condition.

Price ranges on page 160

Left: K*R 101, 21" tall (Richard Wright)
Right: K*R 117A, 28" tall (Jan Foulke)

Mold #101	12-15"	$1,000-1,200
Mold #114	12-15"	1,200-1,500
Mold #115 A	15-16"	1,400-1,600
Mold #116	15-16"	800- 900
Mold #117	19-22"	1,800 up
Mold #117n	15-20"	500
Mold #127	26"	1,000 up

Top left: K*R
114
16" tall
(Helen Teske)

Bottom right:
K*R
118A
16" tall Baby
(H & J Foulke)

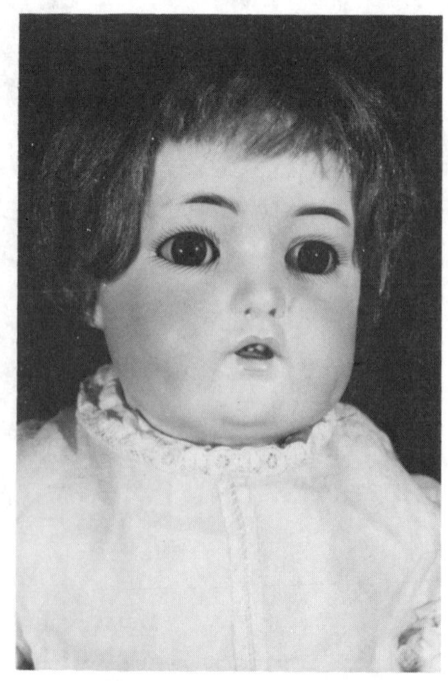

Top left: K * R, 117n 24" tall (Helen Teske)
Top right: K * R, 115A 15" tall (Richard Wright)
Bottom right: K * R, 116A, 24" tall (Richard Wright)

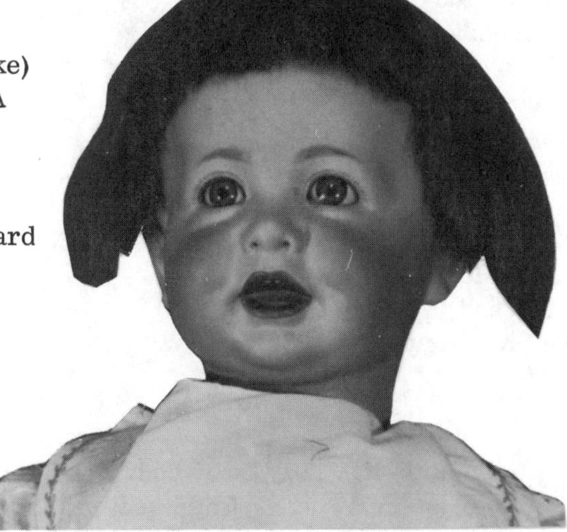

K&R Character Baby and Toddler

MAKER: Kammer & Reinhardt of Waltershausen, Thüringia, Germany
DATE: 1909 - on
MATERIAL: Bisque head, composition bent-limb body or ball-jointed toddler body
SIZE: Various
MARK: "K(star)R", sometimes with numbers, such as 126, 121, 122, 128, "S & H", and many times "Germany"

Marked K(star)R Baby: Bisque head, original or good wig, sleep eyes, open mouth, composition bent-limb body, nicely dressed, may have voice box or spring tongue; all in good condition. Mold #126:
13-15" $225-250*
19-20" $300-325*
24-25" $375-400*

With chubby, jointed toddler body:
14-16" / $300-350*
22-24" / $350-400*

*Allow extra for molds 121, 122, and 128 and for flirty eyes

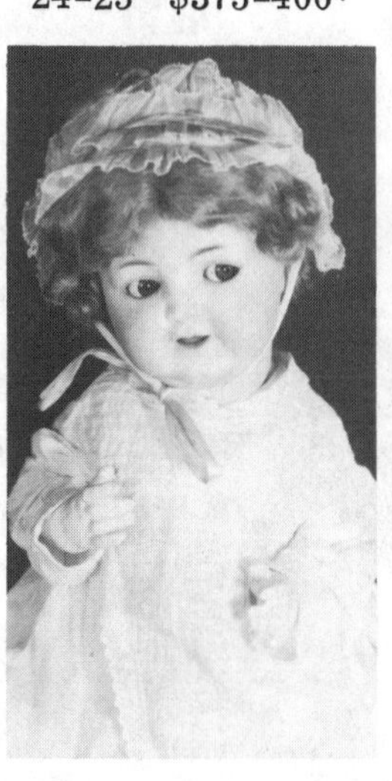

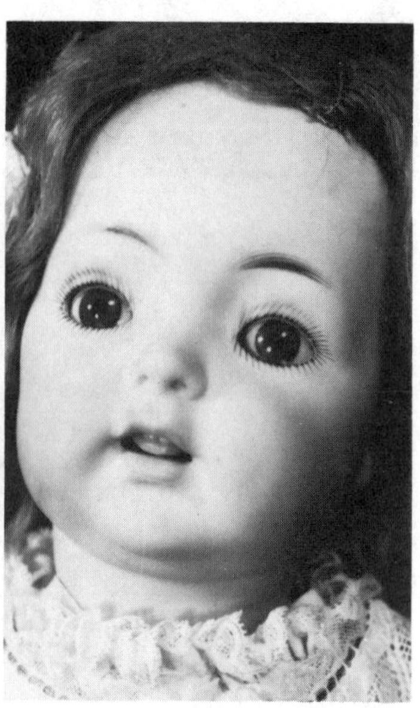

Left: K (star) R / 126 / Baby body / 24" tall / (H&J Foulke)
Right: K (star) R / 121 / Child body / 24" tall / (H&J Foulke)

K & R Child

MAKER: Kämmer & Reinhardt of Waltershausen, Thüringia, Germany
DATE: 1895 began use of "K(star)R" mark
MATERIAL: Bisque head, composition ball-jointed body
SIZE: Various
DESIGNER: Karl Krauser, after 1901
MARK: "K(star)R", sometimes with "S & H", and many times "Germany", often "403"

K & R
SIMON & HALBIG
403

Marked K(star)R Child Doll: Bisque head, original or good wig, sleep eyes, open mouth, pierced ears, dressed, ball-jointed composition body; all in good condition.

7-10"	$ 85-135
17-19"	$165-185
24-27"	$225-250
29-32"	$300-350

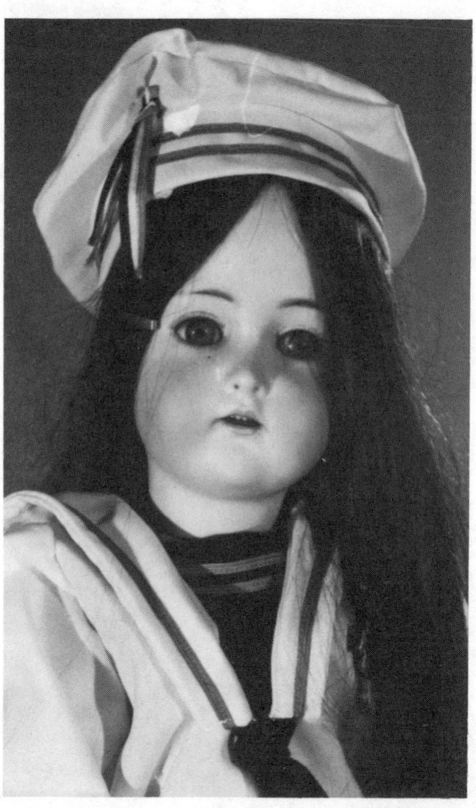

K☆R
Simon & Halbig
403
24" tall
(Helen Teske)

Kaiser Baby

MAKER: Kämmer & Reinhardt of Waltershausen, Thüringia, Germany
DATE: 1909 - on
MATERIAL: Bisque head, composition bent-limb body
SIZE: Various
MARK: "K (star) R #100"

Marked Kaiser Baby: Solid dome bisque head, original composition bent-limb body, intaglio eyes, dressed, open/closed mouth, all in good condition.

Size 11-12" $350-375
Size 14-15" $425

Composition version called "Baby Bumps"

Size 14-15" $ 85- 95

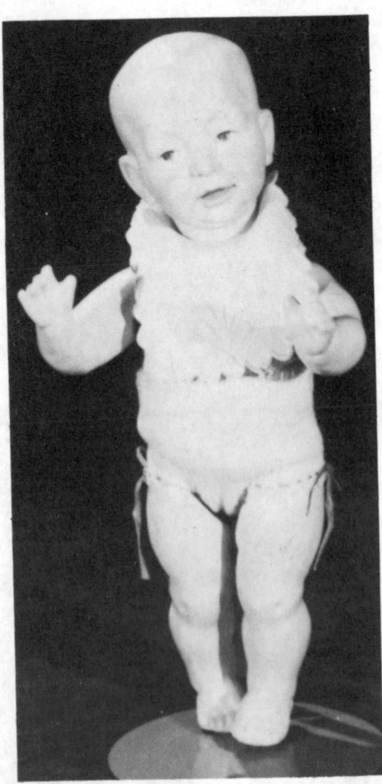

K*R
100
15" tall
(Emily Manning)

Kamkins

MAKER: Louise R. Kampes Studios, Atlantic City, N.J., U.S.A.
DATE: Ca. 1920
MATERIAL: Molded mask face, cloth stuffed torso and limbs
SIZE: Various (about 16" - 19")
MARK: "Kamkins, a dolly made to love.
Patented by L.R. Kampes.
Atlantic City, N.J."

KAMKINS
A DOLLY MADE TO LOVE
PATENTED BY L.R. KAMPES
ATLANTIC CITY, N.J.

Marked "Kamkins": Molded mask face with painted features, wig, cloth body and limbs, dressed, all in good condition.

Size 19" $225-250

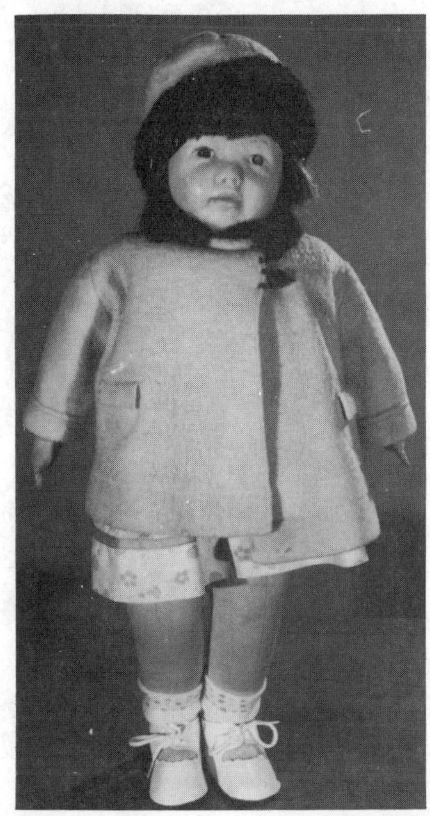

Kamkins signed on foot
Original hat and coat
19" tall
(Helen Teske)

Kate Greenaway

MAKER: Alexander Doll Co., New York, N.Y., U.S.A.
DATE: 1942
MATERIAL: All composition
SIZE: 13", 15", 16", 20", 24"
MARK: "Princess Elizabeth" on head; on dress tag "Kate Greenaway/Madame Alexander, N.Y./All Rights Reserved"

Kate Greenaway: Composition swivel head, blond hair, sleep eyes with lashes, open mouth, composition body, jointed shoulders and hips; original clothes; all in good condition.

Size 15-20" $100-125

Kate Greenaway
20" tall
All original
(Barbara Crescenze)

Kestner Character Baby & Toddler

MAKER: J. D. Kestner, Jr., Waltershausen, Thüringia, Germany
DATE: 1910 - on
MATERIAL: Bisque head, composition bent-limb body
SIZE: Various
MARK: "J.D.K.", sometimes numbers such as 211, 152, 257, 142 and "Germany"

made in
F. Germany. 10
211
J.D.K.

Marked Kestner Baby: Bisque head, molded and/or painted hair or good wig; bent-limb body, open mouth, sleep eyes or set, well dressed; nice condition.

Mold # 152:	Size 10-12"	$150-200	Size 15-19"	$235-275
Mold # 211:	Size 14-16"	$250-350	Size 18-21"	$400-500
Mold # 257:	Size 12-13"	$200-225*	Size 15-17"	$250-275*
Solid Dome:	Size 10-12"	$175-250	Size 14-16"	$250-300
			Size 19-24"	$400-500

* Allow extra for toddler body and flirty eyes.

Left: JDK, 226,Baby Body, 24" tall, (H & J Foulke)
Right: JDK, 260, Toddler Body, 24" tall, (Helen Teske)

Kestner Character Child

MAKER: J.D. Kestner, Jr., Waltershausen, Thüringia, Germany
DATE: 1910 - on
MATERIAL: Bisque head, jointed composition body
SIZE: Various
MARK: Usually only a number

Kestner Character Child: Bisque head character face, painted or glass eyes, closed or open-closed mouth, plaster pate, wig. Good jointed composition body. Dressed. All in good condition.

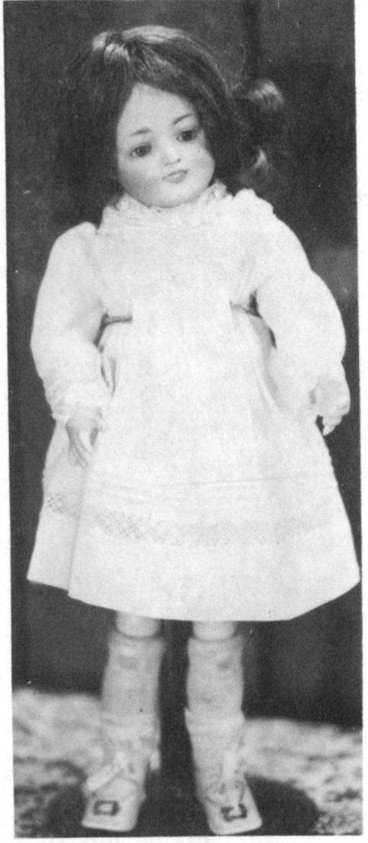

Size 16-19" $450 and up depending upon face.

"151"
Kestner Character
13" tall
(Becky Roberts)

Kestner Child
(Closed Mouth)

MAKER: J.D. Kestner, Jr. of Waltershausen, Thüringia, Germany
DATE: Ca. 1880
MATERIAL: Bisque socket head, ball-jointed composition body or bisque shoulder head on kid body with bisque arms
SIZE: Various
MARK: Sometimes numbers

Kestner Closed-mouth Child: Bisque head, closed mouth, paperweight or sleep eyes, good wig, body as above, well dressed; all in good condition.

Size 16-17" $400-450*
Size 21-22" $475-525*
Size 28-30" $ 650-750*
*Allow extra for character face.

Left: Unmarked Kestner, 16" tall (H & J Foulke)
Right: Unmarked Kestner, character-type, 21" tall (Sue Bear)

Kestner Child Doll
(Open Mouth)

MAKER: J.D. Kestner, Jr., Waltershausen, Thüringia, Germany

DATE: Late 1880's to late 1930's

MATERIAL: Bisque head, jointed composition or kid body

SIZE: Various

MARK: Socket Head - Numbers, such as 171, 146, 164, 195 (see Mark A)
Shoulder Head - Numbers, such as 154, 159 (see Mark A)
Both - A5, B6, C7 and Made in Germany
Composition body - see Mark B
Kid body - Sometimes Mark C

Mark C: J.D.K. Germany

Mark A: made in
D Germany. 8.
162.

Mark B: Excelsior
D.R.P. No. 70686
Germany

Kestner Child doll: Bisque socket head on ball-jointed body; sleep eyes, open mouth, good wig; dressed; all in good condition.

Size 6- 8" $110-165
Size 13" $150
Size 16-19" $150-185
Size 20-24" $200-225
Size 26-27" $250
Size 29-32" $300-350

Bisque shoulder head on jointed kid body; sleep eyes, open mouth, good wig; dressed; all in good condition. Prices as above. Allow extra for swivel neck.

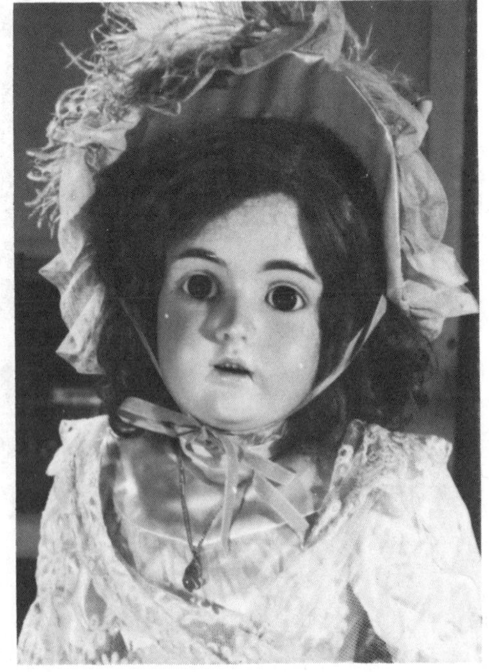

171
Made in Germany
30" tall
(H&J Foulke)

Kestner Gibson Girl

MAKER: J.D. Kestner, Jr. of Waltershausen, Thüringia, Germany
DATE: Ca. 1910
MATERIAL: Bisque shoulder head, kid body
SIZE: Various
MARK: Shoulder head: "Made in Germany" (sometimes "Gibson Girl" on kid body)

Kestner "Gibson Girl": Bisque shoulder head with closed mouth, uplifted chin, glass eyes, good wig. Kid body with bisque lower arms. Beautifully dressed. All in good condition.

Size 10-13" $1,000-1,200
Size 18-22" $1,500-2,000

Gibson Girl
10" tall
(Becky Roberts)

Kewpie®-Bisque
(O'Neill)

MAKER: J.D. Kestner and other Germany companies
DATE: 1913 - on
MATERIAL: All bisque as well as bisque heads for cloth bodies and bisque heads found on chubby toddler ball-jointed composition bodies
SIZE: Various
DESIGNER: Rose O'Neill, U.S.A.
U.S. AGENT: George Borgfeldt & Co., New York, N.Y., U.S.A.
MARK: "O'NEILL" - incised on sole of foot; and/or red and gold heart shape "KEWPIE O'NEILL" label on chest, and/ or round label on back - "Copyright ROSE O'NEILL"

Marked (all-bisque) Kewpie: Standing, legs together, arms jointed, blue wings, painted features, eyes to side. Perfect.

4-6"	$60-85*
7 1/2-9"	$125-165

*Allow extra for action poses and jointed hips

All-bisque Kewpie with label on torso
Rare jointed hips
6" tall
(H&J Foulke)

Kewpie-Celluloid
Ⓣ (O'Neill)

MAKER: Karl Standfuss, Deuben near Dresden, Saxony, Germany
DATE: Ca. 1913 - on
MATERIAL: All celluloid - flesh color
SIZE: Various
DESIGNER: Rose O'Neill, U.S.A.
U.S. AGENT: George Borgfeldt & Co. of New York, N.Y., U.S.A.
MARK: Gummed labels, front or back, etc.

Marked Celluloid Kewpies: Flesh-colored Kewpie, straight standing, arms jointed, has blue wings, legs together; all in mint condition.
Size 2-1/2" to 3-1/2" $20-25
Size 8-10" $65-85

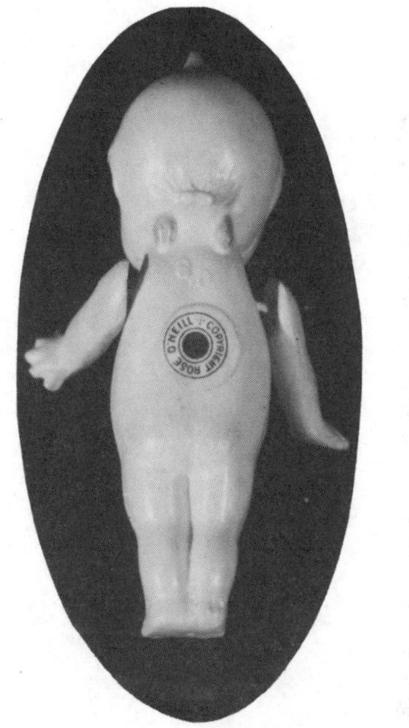

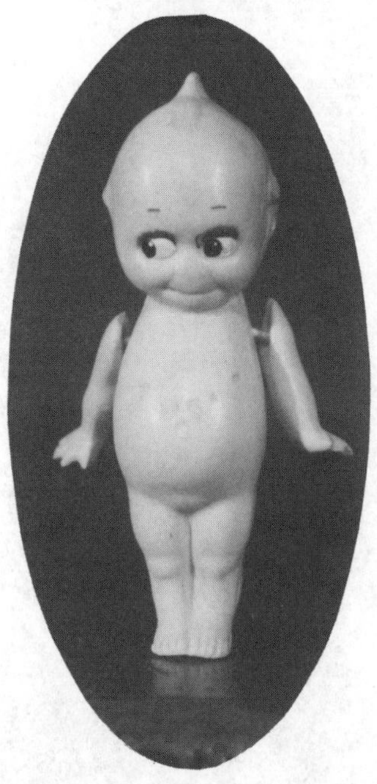

Celluloid Kewpie with sticker, 3-1/2" tall (H & J Foulke).

Kewpie-Composition ®

MAKER: Rex Doll Co., New York, N.Y.; Mutual Doll Co., New York, N.Y.; also Cameo Doll Co., New York, N.Y. (1922), U.S.A.
DATE: Ca. 1913
MATERIAL: Composition
SIZE: Various, usually 12"
DESIGNER: Rose O'Neill, U.S.A.
U.S. AGENT: George Borgfeldt & Co., New York, N.Y., and others
MARKS: Heart-shaped labels on chest etc.

Composition Kewpie: Composition socket head, jointed arms and legs, painted features, dressed. All in good condition.

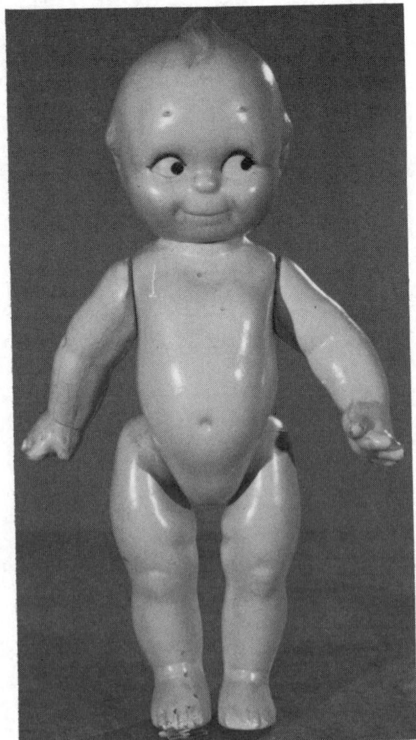

11-13" $65-75

Kewpie
12"
(Jan Foulke)

Kiddiejoy Infant

MAKER: Armand Marseille, Thüringia, Germany for Hitz, Jacobs & Kassler, New York, N.Y., U.S.A.
DATE: 1925 - on
MATERIAL: Bisque head, cloth body
SIZE: 9-1/2 inches up
MARK:

Germany
Kiddiejoy
A 1. M

Marked Kiddiejoy Infant: Bisque head with molded hair, sleep eyes, closed mouth. Cloth body with composition arms and legs. Dressed. All in good condition

10-12" $200-250

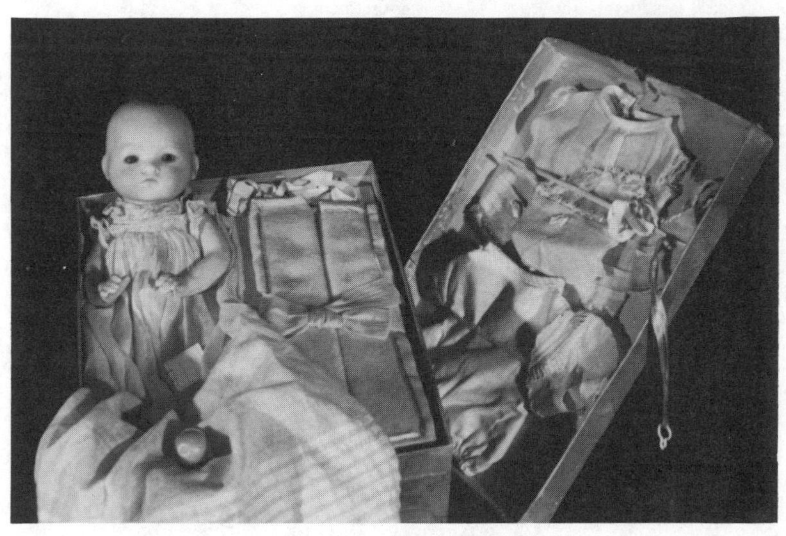

10" Kiddiejoy
In original box
(H&J Foulke)

Kley & Hahn Character Baby

MAKER: Kley & Hahn of Ohrdruf, Thüringia, Germany
DATE: Ca. 1910
MATERIAL: Bisque head, composition bent-limb body
SIZE: Various
MARK: K & H "Germany"; numbers, such as 158, 167, 266

Marked Kley & Hahn Baby: Bisque head, bald or wigged, bent-limb body, sleep or intaglio eyes, open/closed mouth. Fully dressed, all in nice condition. Size 16-21" $350-450

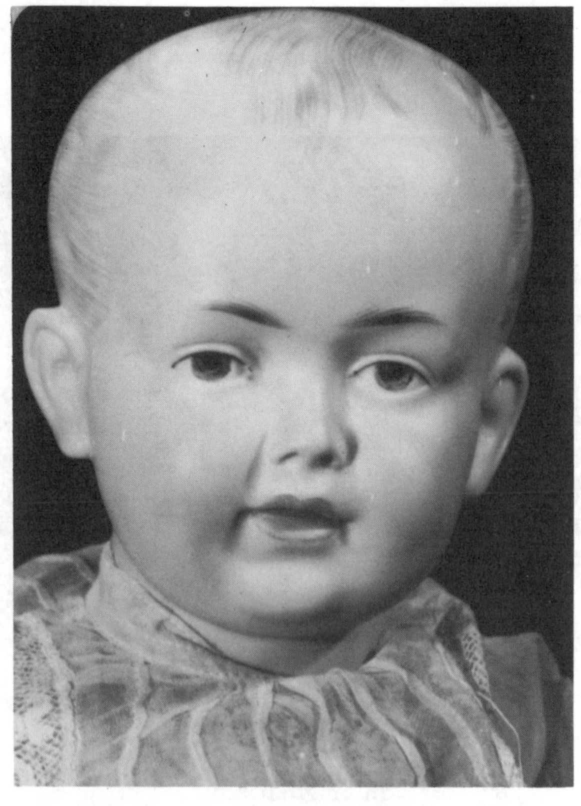

"531", 12" tall, Intaglio eyes, Open/closed mouth, (H & J Foulke)

Kley & Hahn Character Child

MAKER: Kley & Hahn, Ohrdruf, Thüringia, Germany
DATE: Ca. 1910
MATERIAL: Bisque head, jointed composition body
SIZE: Various
MARK: "Germany" and numbers

K&H
Germany

Marked K & H Child: Bisque character face, bald or wigged, sleep or intaglio eyes, closed mouth; jointed composition child or toddler body. Dressed. All in good condition.

Size 12-14" $375 and up*

*Higher price depending upon face.

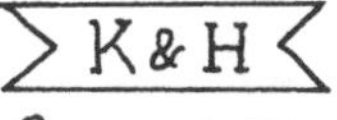

Germany
166-15

So-called Tommy Tucker 28" tall (Also could occur on a jointed composition body) (Clendenien Collection)

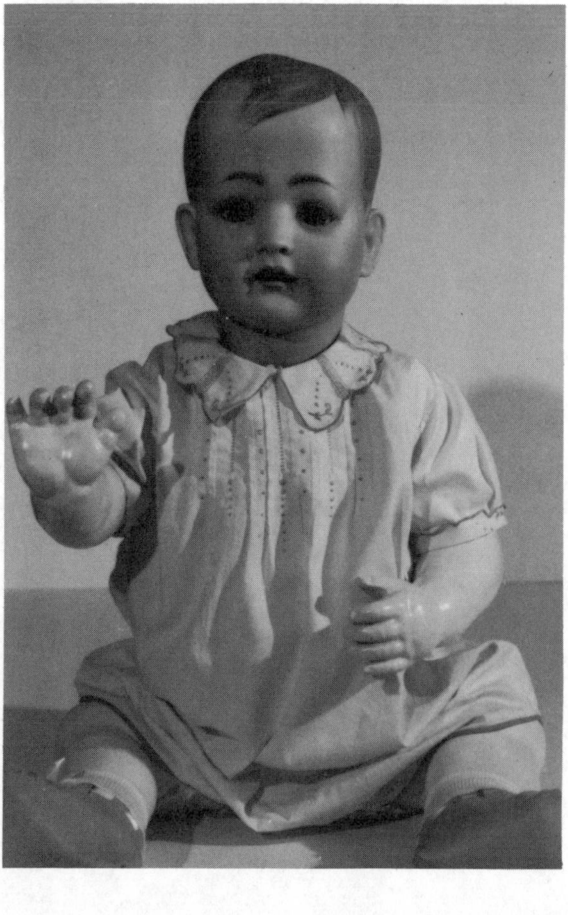

Kling Bisque Head

MAKER: Kling & Co., Ohrdruf, Thüringia, Germany
DATE: 1880 - on
MATERIAL: Bisque shoulder head, cloth body, bisque lower limbs
SIZE: Various
MARK:

Kling Bisque Head: Bisque shoulder head usually with molded hair, painted eyes (sometimes glass), closed mouth; cloth body with bisque lower limbs. Dressed. All in good condition.

Size 15-18" $150-200

Kling-type
13-1/2" tall
(Clendenien Collection)

Krauss

MAKER: Gebrüder Krauss of Eisfeld, Thüringia, Germany
DATE: Ca. 1907
MATERIAL: Bisque head, ball-jointed composition body
SIZE: Various
MARK: Numbers such as 165 and "Germany"

Marked Krauss Doll: Bisque head, ball-jointed body, sleep eyes, open mouth, good mohair wig, dressed, all in good condition.

Size 21-26" $165-195

Krauss doll, original costume, 10" tall (Joyce Alderson)

Käthe Kruse

MAKER: Käthe Kruse, Berlin, Germany
DATE: 1910 - on
MATERIAL: Molded muslin head (hand painted), jointed cloth body
SIZE: Various
MARK: "Käthe Kruse" on sole of foot, sometimes also "Germany" and a number

Käthe Kruse
81971

Made in
Germany

Marked Käthe Kruse: Jointed at shoulders and hips, suitably dressed, in good condition. Size 17" painted hair $300-325

Kathe Kruse
17" tall
All original
(H & J Foulke)

Lanternier Child

MAKER: A. Lanternier & Cie. of Limoges, France
DATE: Ca. 1891 to ca. 1925
MATERIAL: Bisque head, papier-mâché body
SIZE: Various
MARK: Anchor with "Limoges A.L. -- France" or "Fabrication Francaise A.L. & Co. Limoges", sometimes "Cherie", "Favorite", "La Georgienne", "Lorraine"

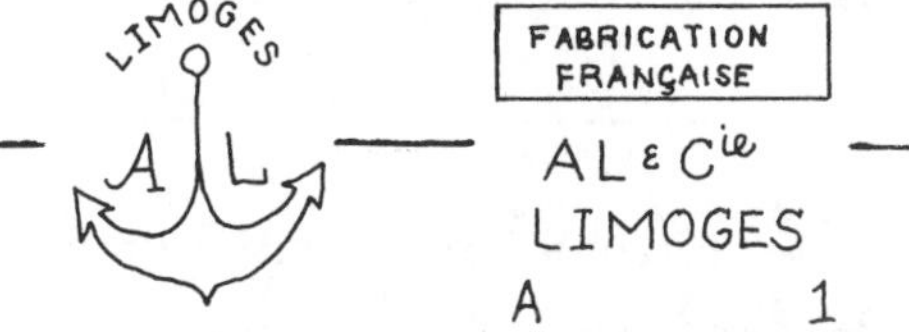

Marked Lanternier Child: Bisque head, papier-mâché jointed body, good or original wig, large stationary eyes, open mouth, pierced ears, pretty clothes; all in good condition.

19-21" $250-350

"La Georgienne"
18" tall
(Joyce Alderson)

Buddy Lee

MAKER: Name of maker kept secret by H. D. Lee Co., Inc. Garment Manufacturers of Kansas City, Missouri, for whom dolls were made.
DATE: 1920 to 1962
MATERIAL: Composition from 1920 to 1948. Hard plastic from 1949 until 1962.
SIZE: 13" only
MARK: "BUDDY LEE" embossed across shoulders

Marked Buddy Lee: Early all-composition; molded, painted eyes and hair; jointed only at shoulders - legs apart; dressed in original Lee clothes. Eyes to side; all in good shape.
Marked Buddy Lee: Later all-hard plastic doll. Mold changed slightly by slimming the legs, making the doll easier to dress and undress. This was done in 1949. Molded painted hair, painted eyes to side; jointed at shoulders; legs apart; dressed in Lee original clothes; all in nice condition.

All Composition 13" $85-100

All Hard Plastic 13" $65-75

All Composition
"Buddy Lee"
13" tall
All original
(Bertha Neumyer)

Terri Lee

MAKER: TERRI LEE Sales Corp., V. Gradwohl, Pres., U.S.A.
DATE: 1946 - Lincoln, Neb.; then Apple Valley, Ca., from 1951 to ca. 1962
MATERIAL: Celanese Plastic (hard plastic)
SIZE: 16 inches only
MARK: "TERRI LEE" embossed across shoulders

Terri Lee Child Doll: 16" marked; all original including clothing and accessories; jointed at neck, shoulders and hips. Mint condition.

Size 16" $40-45
Tiny Terri Lee, 10" tall $30-40

Shelf Group of Terri Lee Dolls with Original Clothes
Photo by Thelma Bateman

Lenci

MAKER: Enrico & Signora Scavini, Italy
DATE: 1920 - on
MATERIAL: Pressed felt head with painted features, jointed felt bodies
SIZE: 5" to 45"
MARK: "LENCI" on cloth and various paper tags

Lenci: All felt (sometimes cloth torso) with swivel head, jointed shoulders and hips. Painted features, eyes usually side-glancing. Original clothes, often of felt or organdy. In very good condition.

Child dolls:	8-9"	$ 55- 65
	12-15"	$135-150
	16-18"	$150-200
	20-24"	$200-250
Lady doll	24-28"	$150-225

14" Lenci, all original
(Beth Foulke)

Little Lady

MAKER: Fleischaker & Baum, New York, N.Y., U.S.A. (EFFanBEE)
DATE: 1939 - 1949
MATERIAL: All composition
SIZE: 15", 18", 19", 22"
MARK: EFFanBEE/Anne Shirley or EFFanBEE/USA embossed on back; paper golden heart on wrist "I am Little Lady"

Little Lady: All composition jointed at neck, shoulders, and hips, separated fingers, mohair wig (some of cotton yarn during WW II), closed mouth, sleeping eyes, original clothes. All in good condition.

Size 15-19" $65-75

Little Lady
with Yarn wig
All original
18" tall
(Barbara Crescenze)

Little Shaver

MAKER: Alexander Doll Co., New York, N.Y., U.S.A.
DATE: 1937
MATERIAL: All cloth
SIZE: Up to 16"
MARK: Cloth dress tag "Little Shaver/Madame Alexander/New York/All Rights Reserved"

Little Shaver: Stuffed pink stocking body, curved arms, tiny waist, mask face with large painted eyes to side, tiny mouth, floss wig glued on; original clothes, all in good condition.
Size 11" $65-75

Little Shaver
11-1/2" tall
(Ann Tardie)

Lori

MAKER: S. & Co., Germany
DATE: After 1910
MATERIAL: Bisque socket head, composition baby body
SIZE: Various
MARK: (GESCHUTZ S & Co GERMANY) (Geschutz Germany) Green stamp

---

Marked "Lori": Solid dome head, painted hair, sleeping eyes, closed mouth. Composition baby body with bent limbs. Dressed. All in good condition. Size 23-28" $1,000-1,200

With open mouth 18-21" $550-650

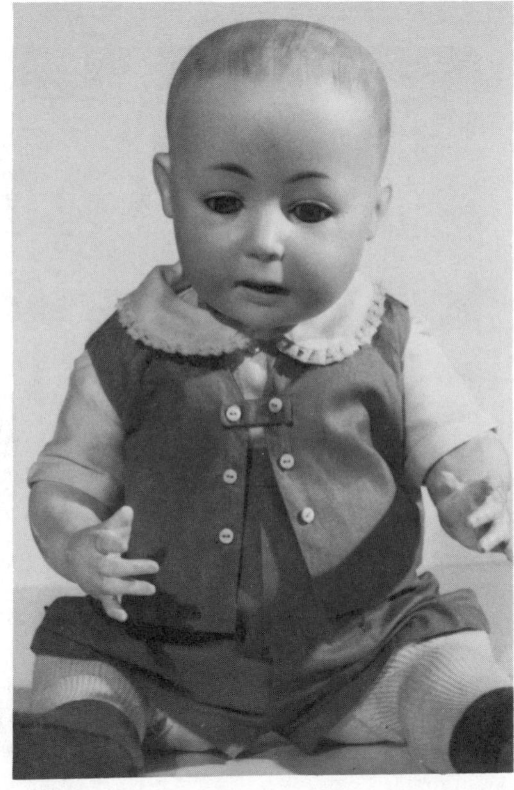

Open-mouth Version of Lori incised only "232" 22" tall (Clendenien Collection)

Lovums

MAKER: Bernard E. Fleischaker and Hugo Baum, New York, N.Y., U.S.A.
DATE: Ca. 1928 to 1939
MATERIAL: Composition head, arms and legs; cloth body
SIZE: Up to 30"
MARK: "LOVUMS" & "EFFanBEE"

EFF AN BEE
LOVUMS
©
PAT. Nº. 1,283,558

Marked Lovums: Composition shoulder head, arms and legs; pretty face, smiling open mouth with teeth, molded painted hair or wig, sleep eyes, cloth body, nicely dressed; all in good condition.

Size 15-20" $55-70

"Lovums"
16" tall
All original
(H & J Foulke)

General Douglas MacArthur

MAKER: Freundlich Novelty Corp. of New York, N.Y., U.S.A.
DATE: Ca. early 1940's
MATERIAL: All composition, molded hat, jointed at shoulders and hips
SIZE: 18 inches
MARK: Tag with "General MacArthur" and manufacturer's name and address etc.

General MacArthur: All composition, molded hat, painted features. One arm made to salute if desired. Original khaki uniform with tags; jointed at shoulders and hips; all in good condition.

Size 18" $95-125

General Douglas MacArthur
18" tall
(H & J Foulke)

Charlie McCarthy
(EFFanBEE)

MAKER: EFFanBEE Doll Corp. (Fleischaker & Baum), New York, N.Y., U.S.A.
DATE: 1937 - on
MATERIAL: Composition head, cloth body
SIZE: Various
MARK: "EDGAR BERGEN'S CHARLIE McCARTHY, an EFFanBEE PRODUCT"

Marked Charlie McCarthy: Composition head, cloth body, strings at back of head to open and close mouth; painted hair and eyes, original clothes, all in good condition.

20" $100-125

Charlie McCarthy
26" tall
(Bertha Neumyer)

Flora McFlimsey

MAKER: Alexander Doll Co., New York, N.Y., U.S.A.
DATE: 1938
MATERIAL: All composition
SIZE: Various
MARK: Head - "Princess Elizabeth
Alexander Doll Co."
Dress tag - "Flora McFlimsey
of Madision Square
by Madame Alexander, N.Y."

Marked Flora McFlimsey: All composition, sleep eyes, open mouth, freckles on nose, human hair wig of red-brown, original clothes; all in good condition.

Size 14-22" $110 up

Alexander
Flora McFlimsey
All original
14" tall
(Beth Foulke)

McGuffey Ana

MAKER: Alexander Doll Co., New York, N.Y., U.S.A.
DATE: 1936
MATERIAL: All composition
SIZE: Various
MARK: On head - "Princess Elizabeth/Alexander"
On dress tag - "McGuffey Ana"

Marked McGuffey Ana: Composition head with sleep eyes, open mouth, human hair or mohair pigtails; composition body jointed at shoulders and hips. Original clothes. All in good condition.

Size 16-18" $ 85-110
Size 20-24" $100-150

Alexander McGuffey Ana
All original
15" tall
(Beth Foulke)

M.B. Character Baby

MAKER: Morimura Bros., a large Japanese import house, New York, N.Y., U.S.A.
DATE: 1915 - 1922
MATERIAL: Bisque head made in Japan, composition baby bodies
SIZE: Various
MARK:

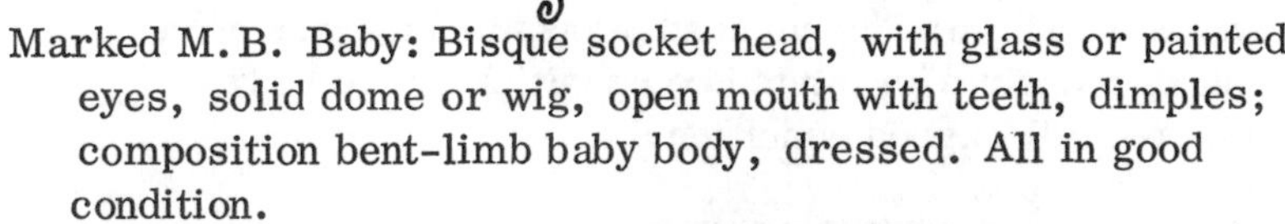

Marked M.B. Baby: Bisque socket head, with glass or painted eyes, solid dome or wig, open mouth with teeth, dimples; composition bent-limb baby body, dressed. All in good condition.

8-10"
$75-100
12-13"
$110-125
16-18"
$135-165

"M.B."
7" tall
(H&J Foulke)

M. B. Child Doll

MAKER: Morimura Bros., large Japanese import house, New York, N.Y., U.S.A.

DATE: 1915 - 1922

MATERIAL: Bisque head made in Japan; jointed composition or kid body

SIZE: Various

MARK:

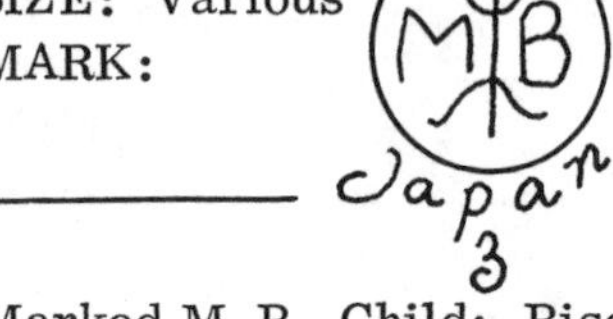

Marked M.B. Child: Bisque head, glass sleep eyes, open mouth, mohair wig; jointed composition or kid body, dressed. All in good condition.

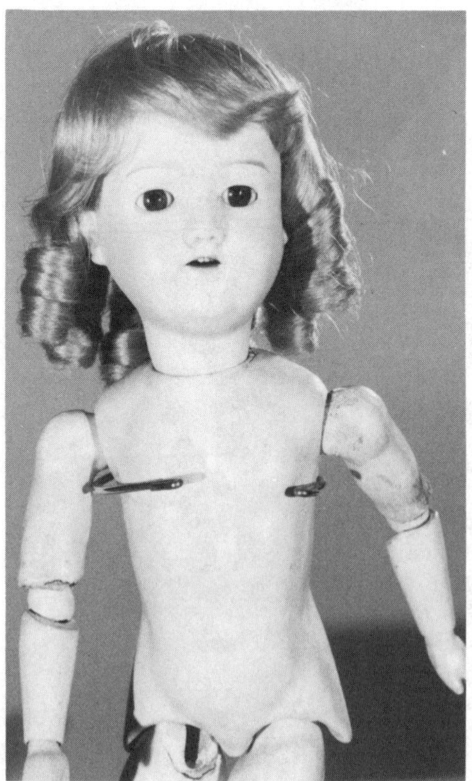

Size 17-19" $125-135
Size 23-25" $150
Size 27-28" $170-180

"M.B." Child
17" tall
(H & J Foulke)

Margie

MAKER: Cameo Doll Co., New York, N.Y., U.S.A.
DATE: 1929
MATERIAL: Composition, segmented wood body
SIZE: 9-1/2" - 10"
DESIGNER: J. L. Kallus
MARK: Red Triangle label on chest: MARGIE/Des. & Copyright/ by Jos. Kallus

---

Margie: Composition head with smiling face; molded hair, painted eyes, closed mouth with painted teeth. Segmented wood body. All in good condition. Undressed.

Size 9-1/2" $75-85

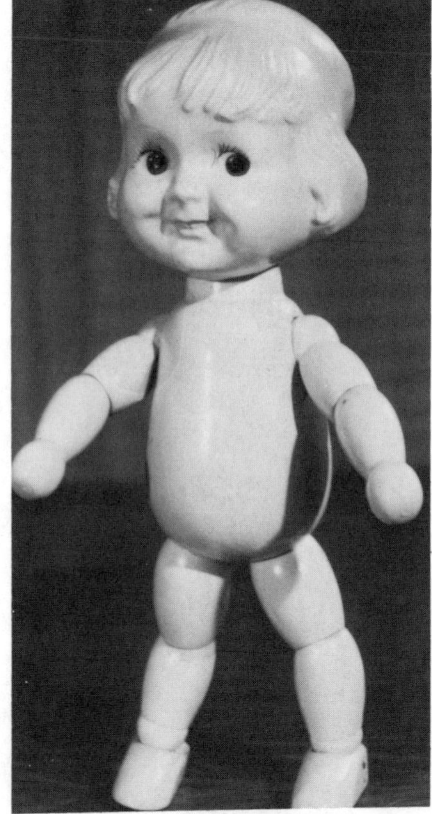

"Margie"
(Mildred Scheer)

Marottes

(Whirling Musical Doll)

MAKER: Various German and French firms
DATE: 1890 - 1921
MATERIAL: Bisque head on wooden stick
SIZE: Usually small
MARK: Various

MAROTTE: Bisque head with glass eyes, good wig, mounted on a wooden stick, plays a musical tune when twirled, fancy hat; all in working condition.

German 11" $135

Marotte
10" tall
(Bertha Neumyer)

Mascotte Bébé

MAKER: May Frères Cie., Paris, France; after 1897 probably merged with Jules Nicholas Steiner
DATE: 1890 - 1901
MATERIAL: Bisque socket head, composition body
SIZE: Various
MARK: Body - BÉBÉ MASCOTTE PARIS Head - MASCOTTE M

Marked "Mascotte": Bisque socket head, glass paperweight eyes, closed mouth, heavy eyebrows, pierced ears, good wig. Jointed composition body, dressed. All in good condition.

Size 20-21" $1050-1150

For photo see, COLLECTOR'S ENCYCLOPEDIA OF DOLLS, the Colemans, p. 60, illustration # 145 A, B & C.

Mason & Taylor
(Wooden Doll)

MAKER: D.M. Smith & Co., Springfield, Vt., U.S.A.
DATE: 1881 to 1893
MATERIAL: Composition heads, wood body, arms and legs. Hands and feet made of pewter or lead. Older type had spoon hands and wooden feet.
SIZE: 12 inches
MARK: None unless black paper band carrying patent dates is still around waist

---

Marked Mason and Taylor Doll: Composition head, wood body, legs and arms; hands and feet usually of metal, fully jointed, dressed; in fair condition.

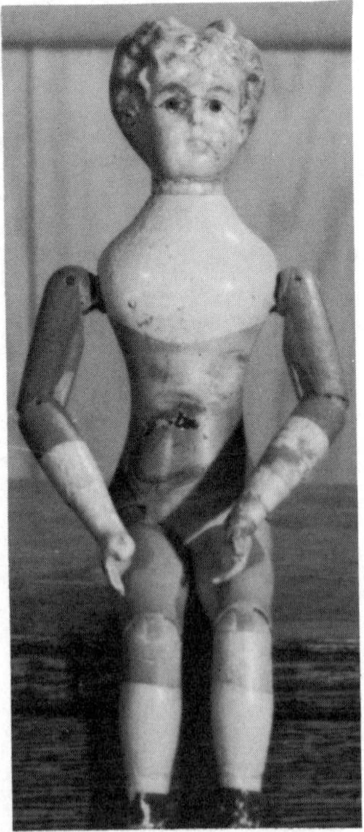

12" $350-400

Mason & Taylor
12" tall
(Bertha Neumyer)

Metal Baby

MAKER: Various U.S. Companies
DATE: Ca. 1920 - on
MATERIAL: All metal
SIZE: Various
MARK: Various

Metal Baby: All metal (with bent limbs) jointed at shoulders and hips with metal springs; molded and painted hair and facial features; painted eyes; closed mouth. Appropriate clothes. All in good condition.

Size 12-14" $50*

*Not enough price samples to justify a reliable range.

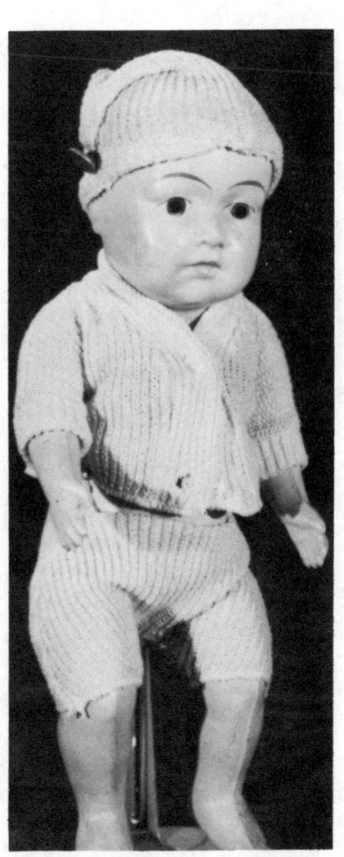

All-Metal
Baby 12" long
Original clothes
(Emily Manning)

Metal Heads

MAKER: Buschow & Beck, Germany (Minerva); Karl Standfuss, Germany (Juno); Alfred Heller, Germany (Diana)
DATE: Ca. 1894 - on
MATERIAL: Metal shoulder head, kid or cloth body
SIZE: Various
MARK:

Marked Metal Head: Metal shoulder head on cloth or kid body, bisque or composition hands, dressed; good condition, not repainted.

With Molded hair and painted eyes. Size 20-21" $55-65

With Molded hair and glass eyes. Size 18-19" $55-65

With wig and glass eyes Size 16-20" $65-75

Minerva with glass eyes and wig Kid body 20" tall (Emily Manning)

Mibs

MAKER: Louis Amberg & Son, New York, N.Y., U.S.A.
DATE: Ca. 1921
MATERIAL: All bisque, composition shoulder head, arms and legs; cloth body
SIZE: Composition - 16 inches; all bisque - 3-6 inches
DESIGNER: Helen Drucker
MARK: All bisque - ©/LA&S 1921/Germany; composition - paper label "Amberg Dolls/Please Love Me/I'm Mibs"

Composition Mibs: Composition shoulder head with molded and painted blond hair, painted blue eyes, closed mouth, wistful expression; cloth body with composition arms and legs; appropriate old clothes; all in good condition. 16" $90-100*

All-bisque Mibs: Molded and painted features, jointed at shoulders and sometimes hips, painted shoes and socks, undressed; all in good condition. Size 3-6" $85 up*

*Not enough price samples to justify a reliable range.

All bisque Mibs
3" tall
(Beth Foulke)

Milliner's Model
(So-called)

MAKER: Unknown German firms
DATE: Ca. 1820's into the 1850's
MATERIAL: Papier-mâché shoulder heads, stiff slender kid bodies, wooden extremities
SIZE: Various
MARK: None

Milliner's Model: Unretouched shoulder head, various molded hairdos, original kid body, wooden arms and legs, painted features, eyes blue, black or brown. Original or very old handmade clothing; entire doll in fair condition.

6-12" $200 and up*
*Price depends upon rarity

Milliner's Model
19" tall
Original clothes
(Bertha Neumeyer)

Carmen Miranda

MAKER: Alexander Doll Co., New York, N.Y., U.S.A.
DATE: 1942
MATERIAL: All composition
SIZE: 7" - 22"
MARK: MME. ALEXANDER on head; "Carmen, Madame Alexander, N.Y., U.S.A. All rights Reserved" on dress label

---

Marked Carmen Miranda: All composition with swivel head, jointed shoulders and hips; sleep eyes, tiny closed mouth, black mohair wig; original clothes including turban and gold-hoop earrings; all in good condition.

11-16" $100 up

Carmen Miranda
11" tall
All original
(Rosemary Dent)

Mon Trésor

MAKER: Henri Rostal, Paris, France
DATE: 1914
MATERIAL: Bisque head, ball-jointed composition body
SIZE: Various
MARK: "Mon Trésor"

Marked "Mon Trésor": Bisque socket head, sleep eyes, open mouth with teeth, good wig, pierced ears, ball-jointed composition body, dressed; all in good condition.

With French body 16-19" $325-425

Monica

MAKER: Monica Doll Studios, Hollywood, Ca., U.S.A.
DATE: 1941 - 1951
MATERIAL: All composition
SIZE: 15", 17", 20", 22", 24"; later 11"
MARK: None

Monica: Composition swivel head, human hair rooted in scalp, painted eyes with eye shadow, closed mouth, composition body with adult-type legs and arms, fingers with painted nails. Dressed. In good condition (nearly all have crazing on faces).

All sizes $85-100

Monica
21" tall
All original
(Helen Teske)

Name Shoulder Heads
(Bisque)

MAKER: Various German firms
DATE: 1890 to World War I
MATERIAL: Bisque shoulder head, jointed kid body; bisque lower arms
SIZE: Various
MARK: Heads incised: "Rosebud", "Lilly", "Daisy", "Alma", "Mabel", "Darling", "Ruth", etc., with numbers and sometimes "Germany"

Name Shoulder Head: Bisque shoulder head marked with doll's name; jointed kid or cloth body, bisque lower arms; well dressed; set eyes, open mouth, good wig; all in good condition.

Size 11-13" $ 85-100
Size 15-18" $115-135

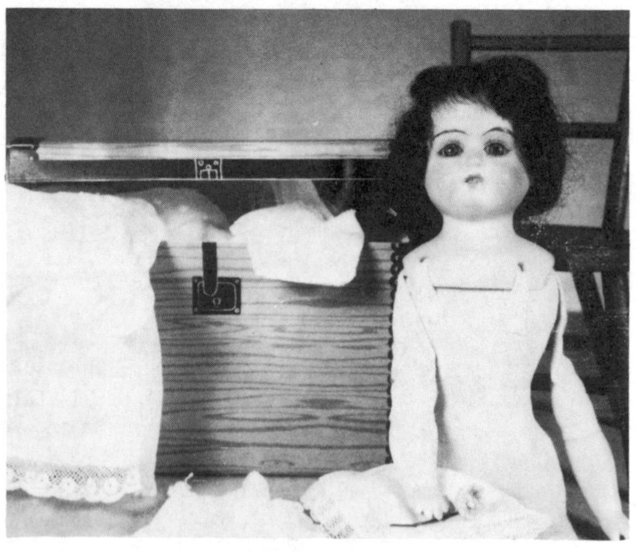

"Ruth" Name shoulder head in script and "18/0",11"
Photo by Thelma Bateman

Nancy

MAKER: Arranbee Doll Co., New York, N.Y., U.S.A.
DATE: Ca. 1930
MATERIAL: All composition or composition swivel shoulder head and limbs on cloth torso.
SIZE: 12" - 20"
MARK: "Arranbee" on head; "Nancy/An Arranbee Doll" on dress tag

---

Nancy: Composition swivel head on body as above, sleep eyes and open mouth with teeth (smaller dolls have painted eyes and closed mouths usually); molded hair or original mohair or human hair wig. Original clothes. All in good condition.

Size 12"	$35-40
Size 16-20"	$50-75

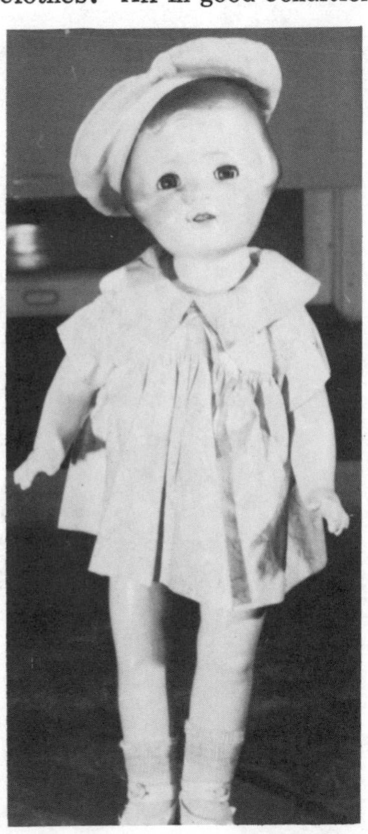

Nancy
All original
(H & J Foulke)

Nancy Ann Storybook

MAKER: Nancy Ann Storybook Dolls Co., South San Francisco, Ca., U.S.A.
DATE: 1941 - on
MATERIAL: Painted bisque; later, plastic
SIZE: About 5-1/2 inches
MARK: Story/Book/Doll/U.S.A. on back; also a wrist tag identifying particular model

---

Marked Storybook Doll: Painted bisque, one piece body, head and legs, jointed arms, mohair wig, painted eyes, original clothes. Good condition. Size 5-1/2" $10-15

"Western Miss"
Original box and clothes.
5-1/2" tall
(Emily Manning)

New Born Babe

(Amberg)

MAKER: Louis Amberg & Son, New York, N.Y., U.S.A.
DATE: 1914; Reissued 1924
MATERIAL: Bisque head, cloth body
SIZE: Various
DESIGNER: Jeno Juszko
MARK: "©L.A. & S. 1914, G 45520 Germany #4" also "Heads copyrighted by LOUIS AMBERG and SON"

New Born Babe: Marked bisque head, cloth body, celluloid, rubber or composition hands; painted bald head, sleep eyes, closed mouth, nicely dressed; all in good condition.

Size 8-10" $165-225
Size 12-14" $275-295

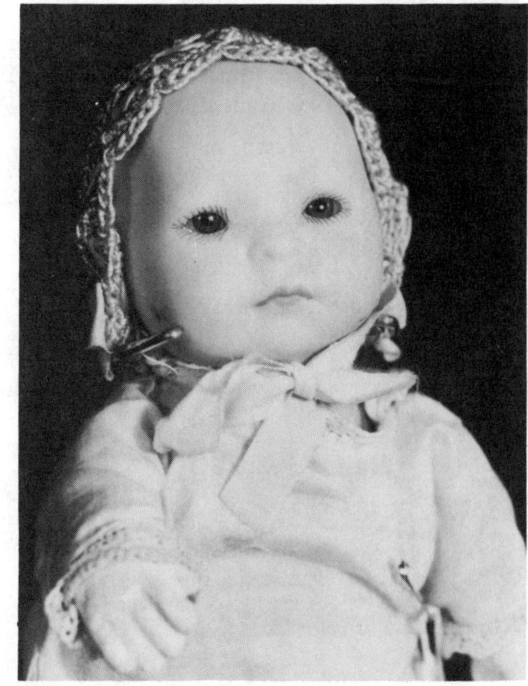

New Born Babe
8" long
(H & J Foulke)

Margaret O'Brien

MAKER: Alexander Doll Co., New York, N.Y., U.S.A.
DATE: 1946
MATERIAL: All composition
SIZES: 14", 18", 21"
MARK: "Alexander" embossed on head and torso;
Dress tag: "Madame Alexander
Margaret O'Brien

Margaret O'Brien: All composition with swivel neck, jointed shoulders and hips. Dark mohair wig in pigtails, sleep eyes, closed mouth. Original clothes. All in good condition.

14"	$100
21"	$125 up

Tagged
"Margaret O'Brien"
All original
14" tall
(Rosemary Dent)

Scarlet O'Hara
(Mme. Alexander)

MAKER: Alexander Doll Co., New York, N.Y., U.S.A.
DATE: 1937
MATERIAL: Composition
SIZE: Various
MARK: Dress tag: "Scarlet O'Hara/Madame Alexander/ N.Y. U.S.A./All rights reserved"

Marked Scarlet O'Hara: All composition jointed at neck, shoulders and hips; original black wig, green sleeping eyes, closed mouth; original clothes, entire doll in fine condition.

18" $165-185

Scarlet O'Hara
All original
18" tall
(Helen Teske)

Oriental Bisque

MAKER: Simon & Halbig, Armand Marseille, J.D. Kestner and other German firms
DATE: 1900 - on
MATERIAL: Bisque head tinted yellow; matching ball-joint or baby body
SIZE: Usually under 20"
MARK: Various for each company

Simon & Halbig, mold #1329 oriental girl	14-16"	$700-800
A.M. #353 bent-limb oriental baby	10-14"	$400-500
JDK Oriental Baby #243	14"	$950 up
Kestner and Bruno Schmidt Girls	20"	$1,000 up

Rare

19" tall
(Richard Wright)

Our Pet

MAKER: Armand Marseille, Köppelsdorf, Thüringia, Germany
DATE: Ca. 1925
MATERIAL: Bisque socket head, composition 5-piece toddler body
SIZE: 9-1/2" - 10"
MARK: TRADEMARK/A Our Pet M/Registered/Germany/ 992 4 0

Marked "Our Pet": Bisque socket head, sleep eyes, open mouth with two upper teeth, wig, composition 5-piece toddler body; dressed; all in good condition.
9-10" $150-165*
*Not enough price samples to justify a reliable range.

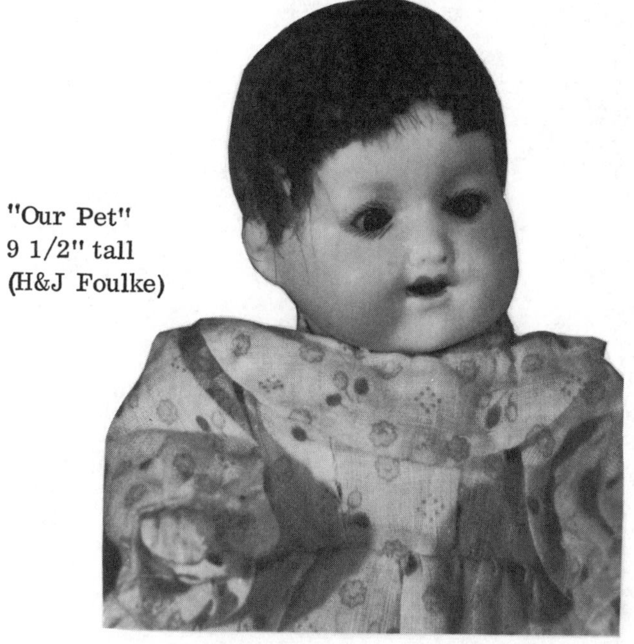

"Our Pet"
9 1/2" tall
(H&J Foulke)

P.M. Character Baby

MAKER: Otto Reinecke of Hof-Moschendorf, Bavaria, Germany
DATE: 1909 - on
MATERIAL: Bisque head, bent-limb composition body
SIZE: Various
MARK: "P M" also PM and numbers, such as 23 and 914, also Germany. (PM for Porzellanfabrik Moschendorf)

PM
914.
Germany
1

Marked Reinecke Baby: Bisque socket head, sleep eyes, open mouth, good wig, 5-piece composition bent-limb baby body. Dressed, all in nice condition.

Size 12-16" $150-200
Size 19-24" $235-265

PM 914
Germany
22" tall
(H & J Foulke)

Painted Bisque
(Tiny Dolls)

MAKER: Various German firms
DATE: Ca. 1930
MATERIAL: All bisque with a layer of flesh colored paint
SIZE: Under 6 inches
MARK: Various

Painted Bisque Tinies: All bisque jointed at shoulders and hips, molded hair, painted features, molded and painted shoes and socks. Dressed or undressed.

Child	3 1/2-4 1/2"	$10-15
Baby	2 1/2"	$12.50

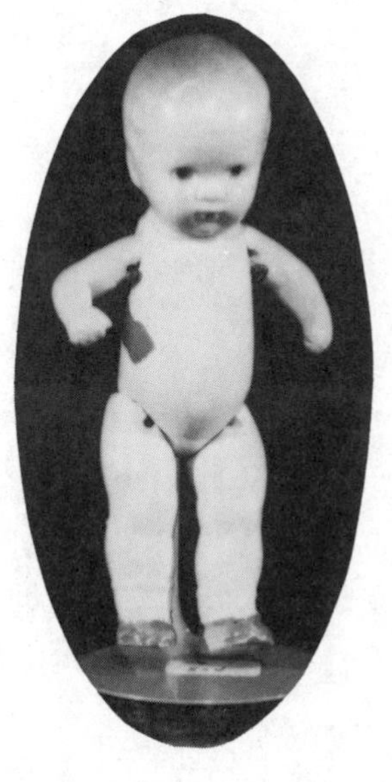

Left: 4 1/2" girl
All original
(H&J Foulke)

Right: 3 1/2" toddler
(H&J Foulke)

Papier-Mâché
(French)

MAKER: Unknown
DATE: Ca. 1825-1860
MATERIAL: Papier-mâché shoulder head, pink kid body
SIZE: Various
MARK: None

French Papier-Mâché: Shoulder head with painted black pate, brush marks around face, nailed on wig (often missing), open mouth with bamboo teeth, pierced nose, set-in glass eyes; pink kid body with stiff arms and legs; appropriate old clothes. All in good condition, showing some wear.

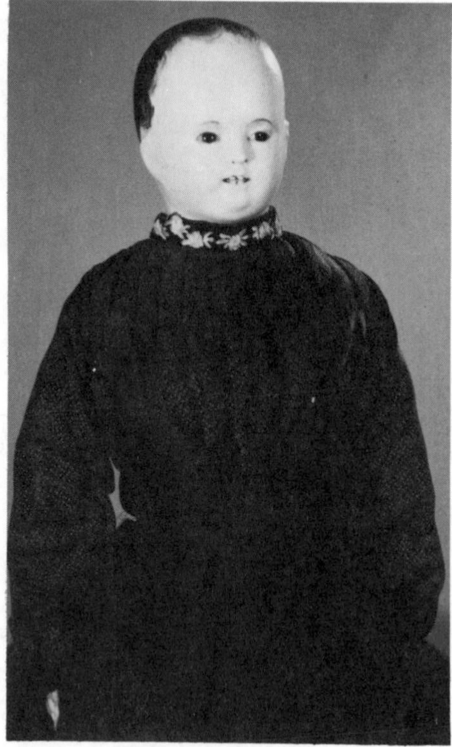

Size 8-12" $275
Size 24-31" $550

French Papier-Mâché
Shoulder Head
24" tall
(Helen Teske)

Papier-Mâché
(German)

MAKER: Various firms
DATE: Ca. 1875 - 1900
MATERIAL: Papier-mâché shoulder head; cloth body, sometimes leather arms
SIZE: Various
MARK: Usually unmarked
Some

A.W.
Ser : a/3

German Papier-Mâché: Shoulder head with molded and painted black or blond hair, painted eyes, closed mouth; cloth body sometimes with leather arms; old or appropriate clothes. All in good condition, showing some wear.

12-13" $75-95
With wig and glass eyes:
18-22" $100-150

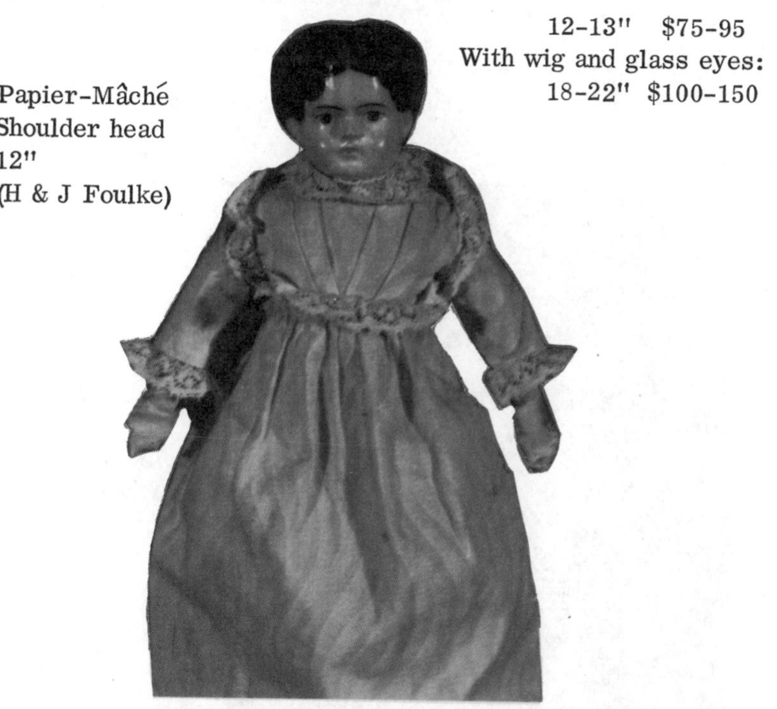

Papier-Mâché
Shoulder head
12"
(H & J Foulke)

Parian

(Untinted Bisque)

MAKER: Various German firms
DATE: Ca. 1860's thru 1870's
MATERIAL: Untinted bisque shoulder head; cloth or kid body; leather, wood, china or combination extremities
SIZE: Various
MARK: None

Unmarked Parian: Pale or untinted shoulder head, sometimes with molded blouse; pierced ears, closed mouth, beautifully molded hairdo, painted eyes, cloth body, lovely clothes; entire doll in fine condition.

	Size 10-14"	$125-185*
	Size 16-18"	$195-225*
Fancy hairdos:	Size 16-18"	$400-450

*Rare with glass eyes and/or swivel neck.
*Allow extra for unusual molded details, such as hair style, flowers or necklace.

Parian with glass eyes, cloth body, leather arms
19" tall
(Joyce Alderson)

Paris Bébé

MAKER: Danel & Cie., Paris, France (Later possibly Jumeau)
DATE: 1889 - 1895
MATERIAL: Bisque socket head, jointed composition body
SIZE: Various
MARK: on body -

on head - TÊTE DÉPOSÉ
PARIS BEBE

PARIS-BEBE
Brévete

Marked Paris Bébé: Bisque socket head, paperweight eyes, pierced ears, closed mouth, good wig, composition jointed body, dressed; all in good condition.

Size 21-24" $750-900
Size 27-28" $1500

For photo see, COLLECTOR'S ENCYCLOPEDIA OF DOLLS by Coleman's, p. 487, illustration 1293.

Parsons-Jackson Baby

MAKER: Parsons-Jackson Co. of Cleveland, Ohio, U.S.A.
DATE: 1910 to 1919
MATERIAL: Biskoline (similar to celluloid) jointed with steel springs
SIZE: Various
MARKS: Embossed figure of small stork on back of head and also on back of shoulders with "PARSONS-JACKSON, CLEVELAND, OHIO" under that.

on head- on body-

TRADEMARK
PARSONS-JACKSON CO.
CLEVELAND, OHIO.

Marked Parsons-Jackson Baby: Socket head and bent-limb baby body of Biskoline; molded-painted hair, painted eyes, spring joint construction. Nicely dressed; all in good condition.

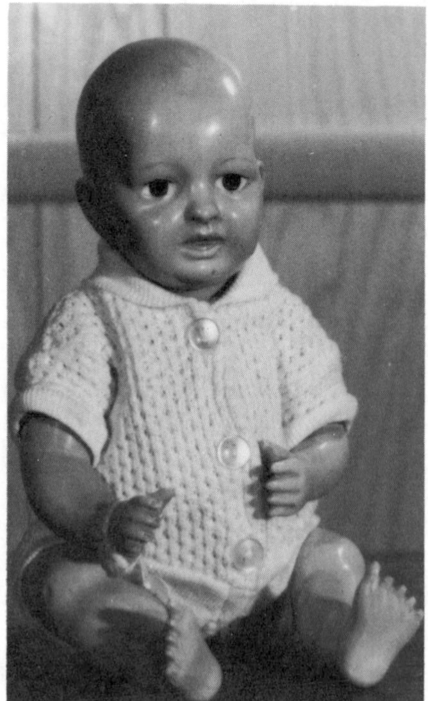

12" $85-110

Parsons-Jackson
11" tall
(Bertha Neumyer)

Patsy Dolls
(EFFanBEE)

MAKER: EFFanBEE Doll Co., New York, N.Y., U.S.A. (Bernard Fleischaker & Hugo Baum)
DATE: 1926 - on
MATERIAL: Composition, jointed at neck, shoulders and hips
SIZE: 5-1/2" - 22"
DESIGNER: Bernard Lipfert
MARK: "EFFanBEE" across back of shoulders, also "Patsy Lou", "Patsy-Ann", "Patsy Joan", "Wee Patsy" etc.

Marked Patsy: All composition, sleep eyes, closed mouth, molded hair. Nicely dressed. Good condition.

5-1/2" Wee Patsy	$100	14" Patricia	$ 60-70
8" Baby Tinyette	$ 50-55	16" Patsy Joan	$ 65-75
8" Patsy Babyette	$ 45-55	19" Patsy Ann	$ 65-75
9" Patsyette	$ 45-55	22" Patsy Lou	$ 80-90
10" Patsy Baby	$ 50-55	26" Patsy Ruth	$125 plus
11" Patsy Jr.	$ 50-60	30" Patsy Mae	$125 plus
14" Patsy	$ 55-65		

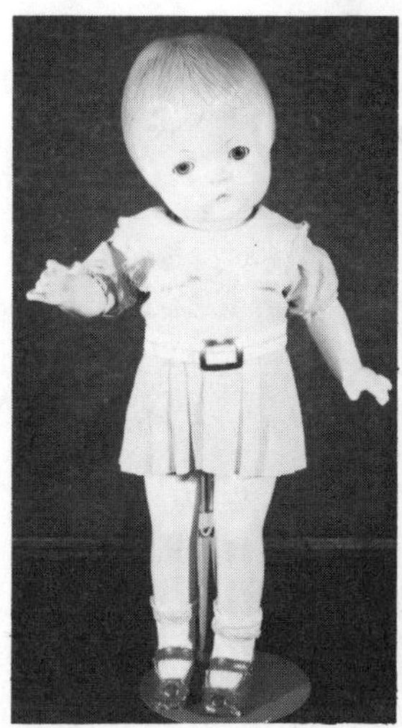

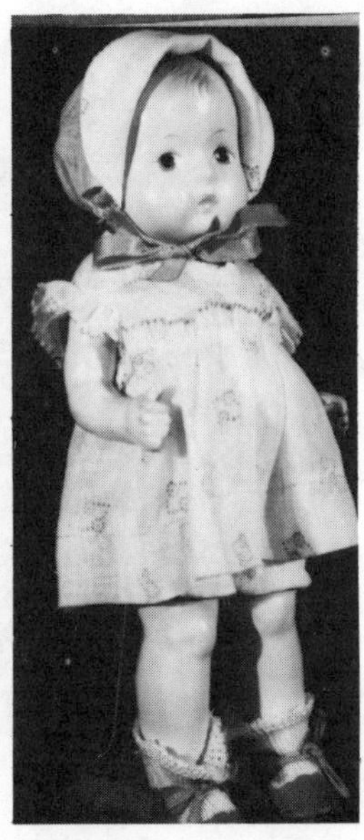

Left: "Patsy Joan" 16" tall, all original. (H & J Foulke)

Right: "Baby Tinyette", with straight legs, 8" tall (H & J Foulke)

Penny Wooden or Dutch Dolls

MAKER: Various German and English Craftsmen
DATE: Late 18th to early 20th century
MATERIAL: All wood, ball-jointed or pegged
SIZE: One-half inch up
MARK: None

Late 18th and Early 19th Century: Finely carved wooden head, glass eyes, wig or carved and painted hair, jointed wooden body. *These are seldom available and could cost $1,000 or more.

Mid - Late 19th Century: Carved wooden head, painted hair and eyes, jointed wooden body, dressed; in good condition.
9-15" $75-150

Early 20th Century: Wooden head, painted hair, eyes and features, carved nose, peg-jointed at shoulders, elbows, hips and knees, dressed; in good condition. $8-30

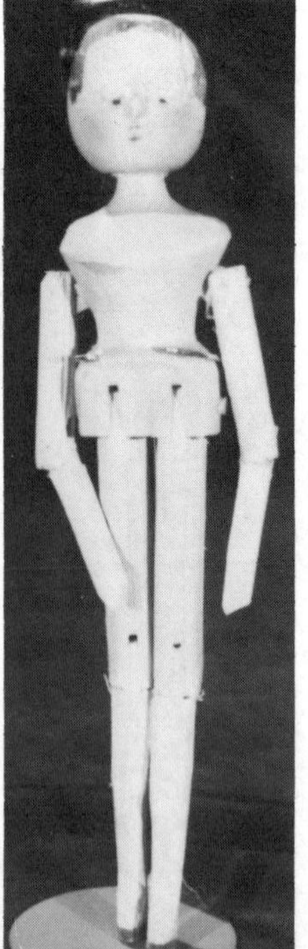

Early 20th Century
Penny Wooden
12" tall
(Emily Manning)

Phénix Bébé

MAKER: Henri Alexandre, Paris, France; Tourrel; Jules Steiner; Jules Mettais

DATE: 1889 - 1900

MATERIAL: Bisque head, jointed composition body (sometimes one-piece arms and legs)

SIZE: Various

DESIGNER: Henri Alexandre

MARK: (BÉBÉ PHÉNIX) PHÉNIX-BABY PHÉNIX ★95

Marked Bébé Phénix: Beautiful bisque head, French jointed body, closed mouth, pierced ears, lovely old wig, bulbous set eyes, well dressed; all in good condition.

Size 23-26" $825-975

Same as above with open mouth 18-21" $475-575

For photo see, COLLECTOR'S ENCYCLOPEDIA OF DOLLS, The Colemans, p. 63, illustration 159 A, B & C

Philadelphia Baby

MAKER: J.B. Sheppard & Co., Philadelphia, Penn., U.S.A.
DATE: Ca. 1900
MATERIAL: All cloth
SIZE: 18" - 22"
MARK: None

Philadelphia Baby: All cloth with treated shoulder-type head, lower arms and legs. Painted hair, well-molded facial features, ears. Stocking body. Fair condition only, showing much wear. Size 21" $350-375

Philadelphia Baby
21" tall
(H & J Foulke)

Piano Baby

MAKER: Gebrüder Heubach, Kestner and other makers
DATE: 1880 - on
MATERIAL: All bisque
SIZE: Usually under 12", some larger
MARK: Many unsigned; some with maker's particular mark

Piano Baby: All bisque immobile with molded clothes and painted features, made in various sitting and lying positions.

3-4" long $35-45
6-7" long $75-85

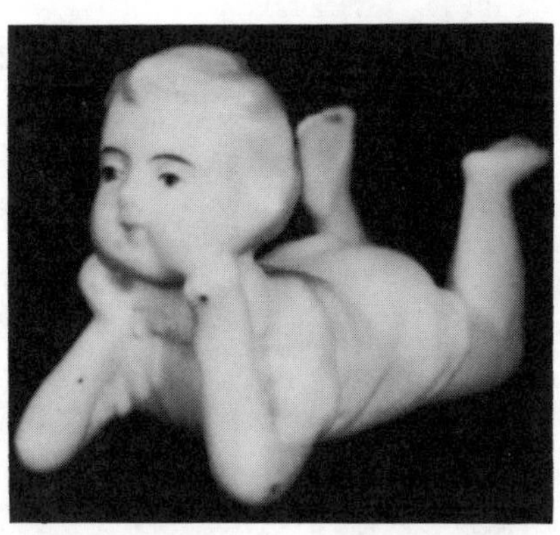

Small Unmarked
Piano Baby
3" long
(H&J Foulke)

Pincushion Dolls

MAKER: Various German firms
DATE: 1900 - on
MATERIAL: China
SIZE: Up to about 7"
MARK: "Germany" and numbers

Pincushions: China half figures with molded hair and painted features, usually with molded clothes, hats, lovely modeling and painting.

Ordinary, arms close	$12 up
Arms somewhat extended	$25 up
Arms very extended, larger size	$55 up

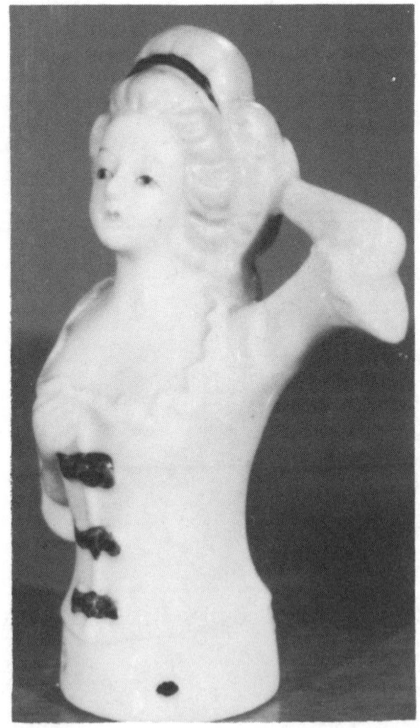

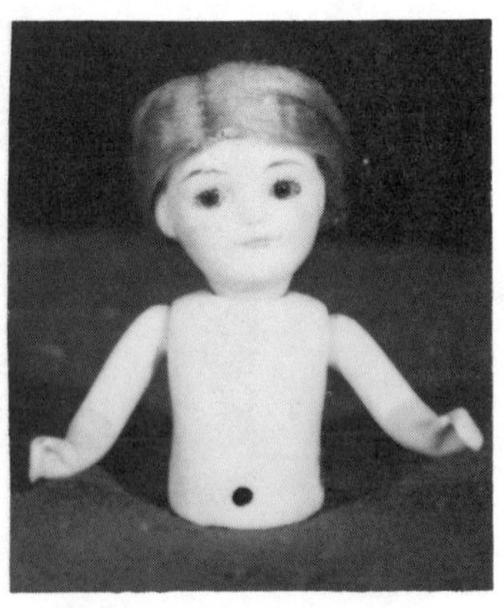

Right: Rare type
2-1/2" tall
(Mike White)

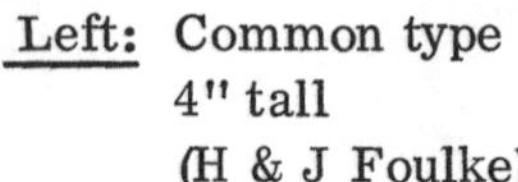

Left: Common type
4" tall
(H & J Foulke)

Pre-Greiner
(So-called)

MAKER: Unknown U.S. firm
DATE: First half of 1800's
MATERIAL: Papier-mâché shoulder head; stuffed cloth body, mostly homemade, wood, leather or cloth extremities
SIZE: Various
MARK: None

Unmarked Pre-Greiner: Papier-mâché shoulder head; painted black hair, center part; vertical curls in back, pupil-less black glass eyes. Cloth stuffed body, leather extremities, dressed in good old or original clothes; all in good condition.
27-32" $600-700*
*Not enough price samples to justify a reliable range.

Same as above with painted eyes: 21-24" $275-375
27-32" $475

Pre-Greiner: 28 inch
Photo by Thelma Bateman

Princess Elizabeth

(Mme. Alexander)

MAKER: Alexander Doll Co. of New York, N.Y., U.S.A.
DATE: 1937
MATERIAL: Composition
SIZE: Various
MARK: "Princess Elizabeth" on back of head and "Alexander Doll Co." underneath. Tag on clothes. (Look carefully. The P.E. mold was used for other Alexander Dolls.)

Marked Princess Elizabeth: Composition head and body, jointed at neck, hips and shoulders; sleep eyes, open mouth, original blond mohair wig, original clothes; all in good condition.

Size 13-17" $65-85

"Princess Elizabeth"
18" tall
Redressed
(Bertha Neumyer)

Puggy

MAKER: American Character Doll Co., New York, N.Y., U.S.A.
DATE: Shown in 1931 catalogue
MATERIAL: All composition
SIZE: About 12"
MARK: "A Petite Doll"

Puggy: All composition chubby body jointed at neck, shoulders and hips. Molded and painted hair, painted eyes to side, pug nose, frowning face, closed mouth, appropriate clothes. All in good condition.

12" $100-125

Puggy
12" tall
(Becky Roberts)

Queen Louise

(A.M.)

MAKER: Thought to be made by Armand Marseille of Köppelsdorf, Thüringia, Germany, for Louis Wolf & Co., Boston, Mass. and New York, N.Y., U.S.A.

DATE: 1910

MATERIAL: Bisque head, composition ball-jointed body

SIZE: Various

MARK: "QUEEN LOUISE -- GERMANY"

Germany
Queen Louise

Marked Queen Louise: Bisque socket head, ball-jointed composition body, good wig, blue, gray or brown sleep eyes; open mouth, good clothing; entire doll in fine condition.

Size 23-26" $150-200

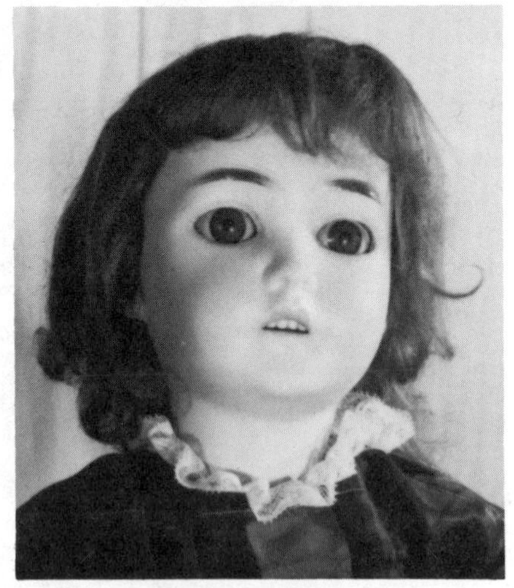

"Queen Louise"
25" tall
(Bertha Neumyer)

R.A. Character Doll

MAKER: Th. Recknagel of Alexandrinenthal, Thüringia, Germany
DATE: 1909 until World War I
MATERIAL: Bisque head, composition bent-limb baby body
SIZE: Various
MARK: "R.A. and Germany" or possibly

R.A. Baby or Toddler: Bisque socket head; composition bent-limb baby or straight-leg curved-arm toddler body; sleeping or set eyes. Nicely dressed; all in good condition

8" $100-135

"Germany R 138 A" / 8" tall / (Richard Wright)

R.A. Child Doll

MAKER: Th. Recknagel of Alexandrinenthal, Thüringia, Germany
DATE: 1886 to ca. World War I
MATERIAL: Bisque head, composition or wood jointed body
SIZE: Various
MARK: "R.A." with numbers and sometimes "Germany"

R.A. Child Doll: Marked bisque head, jointed composition or wooden body, set or sleep eyes, good wig; some dolls with molded painted shoes and socks; all in good condition.

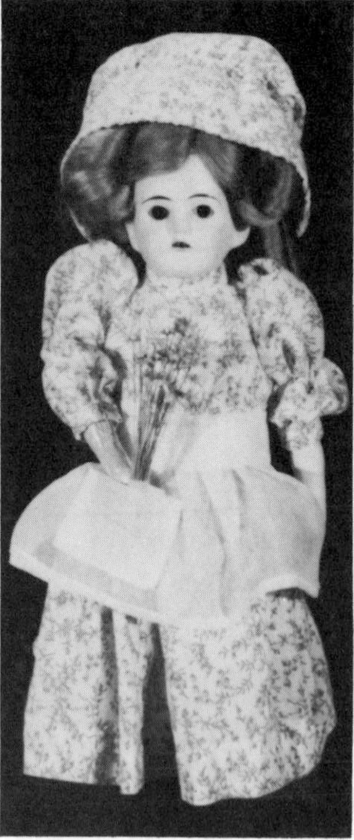

14-16" $110-135

R.A. type
12" tall
(Emily Manning)

R.D. Bébé

MAKER: Rabery and Delphieu of Paris, France
DATE: 1856 (founded) to 1899 - then with S.F.B.J.
MATERIAL: Bisque head, papier-mâché body
SIZE: Various
MARK: "R.D." (from 1890)

Marked R.D. Bébé: Bisque head, jointed papier-mâché body, lovely wig, paperweight eyes, closed mouth, beautifully dressed; entire doll in nice condition.

Closed mouth	15-16"	$650-725
	22-24"	$800-900
Open mouth	18-20"	$400-450
Open mouth with two rows teeth	25"	$675-750

"R.D."
20" tall
(H & J Foulke)

Raleigh Doll

MAKER: Jessie McCutcheon Raleigh, Chicago, Illinois.
DATE: 1916-1920
MATERIAL: Composition heads, cloth bodies or all composition.
SIZE: Various
MARK: No mark

Raleigh Doll: Composition head, molded hair or wig, sleep or painted eyes; composition or cloth body. Appropriate clothes. All in good condition. Size 13-18" $65-95

For photo see, DIMPLES & SAWDUST Volume II, Cooper, p. 167
MORE TWENTIETH CENTURY DOLLS, Anderton, page 1043 to 1050.

Ravca Doll

MAKER: Bernard Ravca, Paris, France. Later (1939) New York, N.Y., U.S.A.
DATE: 1924 - on
MATERIAL: Cloth with stockinet faces
SIZE: Various
MARK: Paper Label: Original Ravca Fabrication Française

Ravca Doll: Stockinet face individually sculpted; cloth bodies and limbs; originally dressed; all in good condition.

7 1/2-10 1/2"	$85-100
18-22"	$135-165

Ravca
French Peasants
10" tall
All original
(H&J Foulke)

Reliable Doll

MAKER: Reliable Toy Co., Toronto, Canada
DATE: 1920 - on
MATERIAL: All composition
SIZE: Usually about 12 inches
MARK: RELIABLE
MADE IN
CANADA

Reliable Doll: All composition jointed at shoulders and hips; molded and painted hair and features; original clothes. In good condition.

Size 13" $30-35

Reliable
Indian
All original
13" tall
(H & J Foulke)

Revalo Child Doll

MAKER: Gebrüder Ohlhaver, Thüringia, Germany
DATE: 1921 - on
MATERIAL: Bisque socket head, ball-jointed composition body
SIZE: Various
MARK:

Revalo
Germany
3

Marked Revalo: Bisque socket head, sleeping eyes, hair eyelashes, painted lower lashes, open mouth, good wig; ball-jointed composition body; dressed; all in good condition.

Size 16-20" $150-175
Size 22-24" $200-225

Unmarked Revalo
17" tall
(Mildred Scheer)

Rohmer Fashion

MAKER: Mademoiselle Marie Rohmer, Paris, France
DATE: 1866 to 1880
MATERIAL: China or bisque shoulder head, jointed kid body
SIZE: Various
MARK:

Rohmer Fashion: China or bisque swivel shoulder head; jointed kid body, set glass eyes, bisque or china arms, kid or china legs, closed mouth, some ears pierced, lovely wig, fine costuming; entire doll in good condition.

16-18" $1500 and up

Rohmer-type
China head
20" tall
(Helen Teske)

Rosebud

MAKER: E.I. Horsman Co., New York, N.Y., U.S.A.
DATE: Ca. 1928
MATERIAL: Composition head and limbs, cloth torso
SIZE: 18 inches
MARK: "Rosebud" embossed on head

Marked Rosebud: Composition swivel head, smiling face with dimples, open mouth with teeth, tin sleep eyes, mohair wig, cloth torso, composition arms and legs, original clothes; all in good condition.

18-22" $40-50

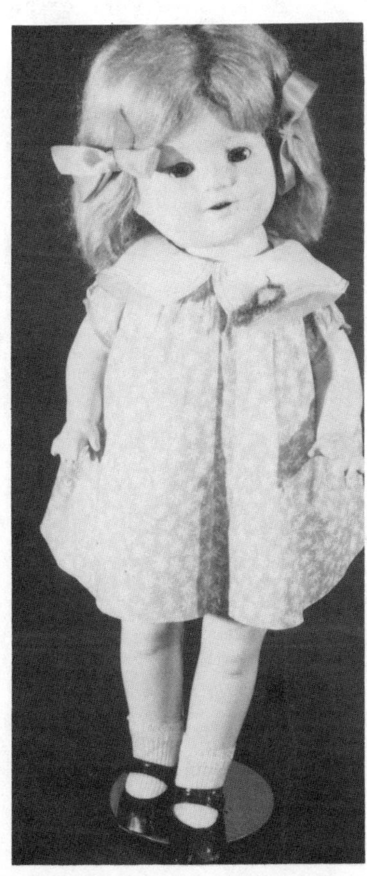

Rosebud
18"
(H&J Foulke)

Rosemary

MAKER: EFFanBEE Doll Co., New York, N.Y., U.S.A. (Fleischaker & Baum)
DATE: Ca. 1925
MATERIAL: Composition shoulder head, arms and legs; cloth torso
SIZE: Various
MARK:

Marked Rosemary: Composition shoulder head, human hair wig, open mouth, tin sleep eyes; cloth torso, composition arms and legs; original or old clothes; all in good condition.

18" $65-75

Rosemary
16" tall
Original
(H&J Foulke)

S.F.B.J. Character Dolls

MAKER: Société Francaise de Fabrication de Bébés & Jouets, Paris, France
DATE: 1910 - on
MATERIAL: Bisque head, composition body
SIZE: Various
MARK: "S.F.B.J. Paris" and number

S.F.B.J
236
PARIS

S.F.B.J. Character Child: Marked bisque head, composition body, nicely dressed; all in good condition.

Mold # 236: 12-15" $400-450
19-21" $550-650*
*Allow extra for toddler body.
Mold # 251:
19-22" $650-750
Mold # 247:
6- 7" $425-500
20" $1400
Mold # 252:
15-21" $2,000-3,000
Mold # 226, 237:
14-16" $950 up
Mold # 235 :
13-15" $700-800

Right: SFBJ
236
Paris
15" tall
Toddler body
(H & J Foulke)

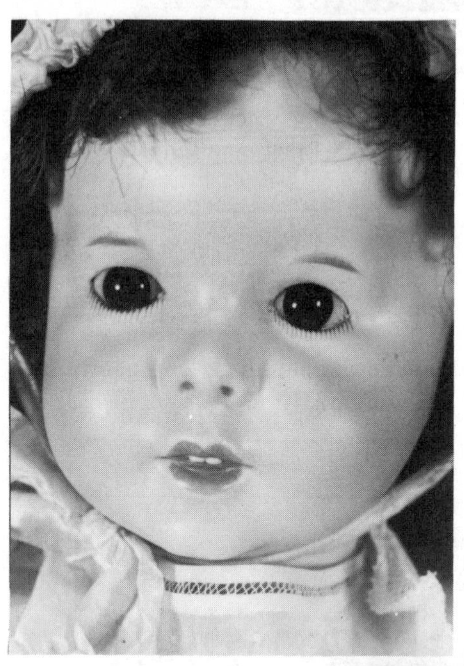

Left: SFBJ
247
Paris
21" tall
Baby body
(Richard Wright)

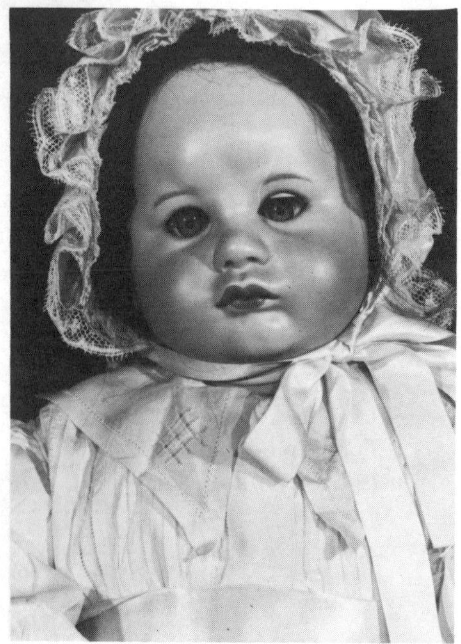

Right: SFBJ
252
Paris
26" tall
Toddler body
(Richard Wright)

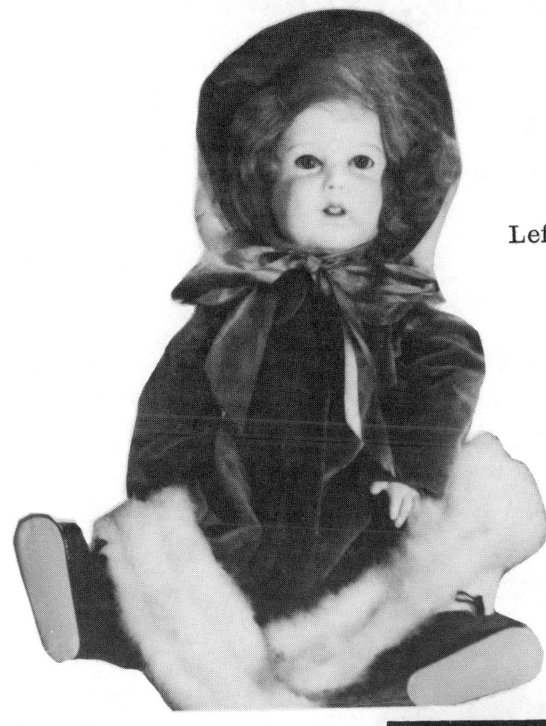

Left: SFBJ
251
Paris
18" tall
Toddler body
(Bertha Neumyer)

Right: Brown and
white bisque,
both marked,
SFBJ 235
(Richard Wright)

S.F.B.J. Child

MAKER: Société Française de Fabrication de Bébés & Jouets, Paris, France
DATE: 1899 - on
MATERIAL: Bisque head, jointed papier-mâché body
SIZE: Various
MARK: "SFBJ Paris"

S.F.B.J
301
PARIS

S.F.B.J. Child Doll: Marked bisque head, jointed composition body, pierced ears, sleep eyes, open mouth, good French wig, nicely dressed, all in good condition.

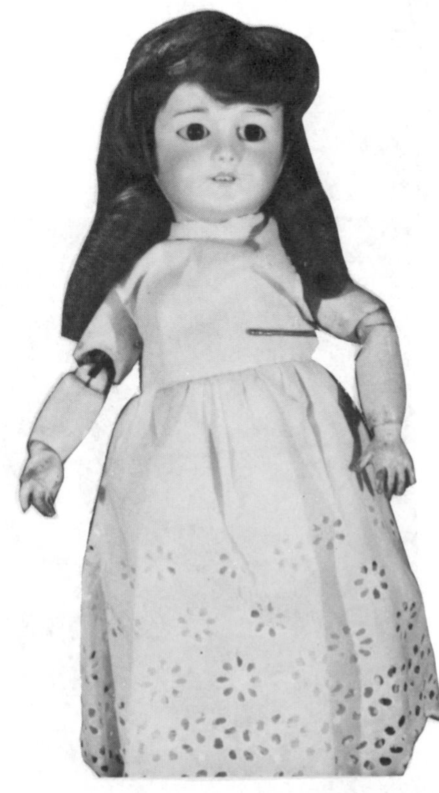

#301 or No number	
20-23"	$300-350
#60	
14-17"	$200-275
19-20"	$275-300

"SFBJ 301 Paris"
20" tall
(Emily Manning)

S.F.B.J. Kiss Throwing & Walking

MAKER: Société Française de Fabrication de Bébés & Jouets, Paris, France
DATE: 1905 - on
MATERIAL: Bisque head, papier-mâché body
SIZE: Various
MARK: "S.F.B.J. Paris" and #301

FRANCE
S.F.B.J.
301
PARIS
2/0

S.F.B.J. Walking-& Kiss-Throwing: Marked bisque head, composition body with straight legs, walking mechanism at top, hand raises to throw a kiss, head moves from side to side, eyes flirt, glass eyes, good wig, open mouth, pierced ears, nicely dressed; all in working order.

21-23" $375-475

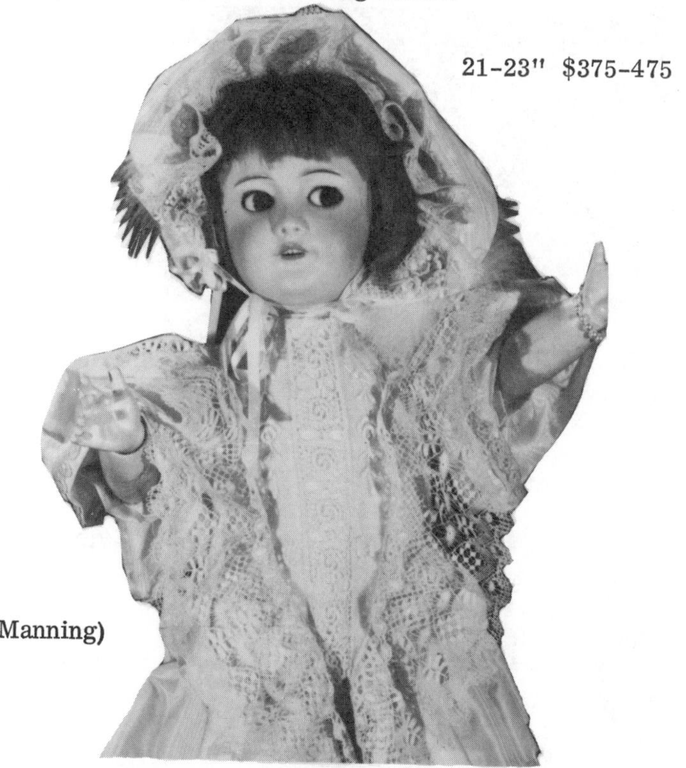

"Unis
301"
22" tall
(Emily Manning)

Santa
(S & H 1249)

MAKER: Simon & Halbig, Gräfenhain, Thüringia, Germany for Hamburger & Co., Berlin, Nürnberg and New York, N.Y.
DATE: 1900-1910
MATERIAL: Bisque socket head, jointed composition body
SIZE: 10-1/2" up
MARK: S H 1249 DEP.
Germany
12

SANTA

Marked S & H 1249: Bisque socket head, open mouth, glass sleeping eyes, pierced ears, good wig, composition ball-jointed body; appropriate clothes; all in good condition.

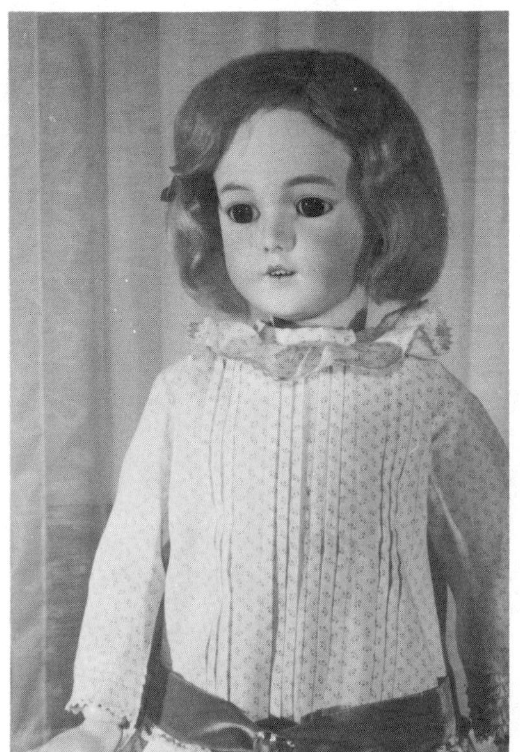

15-18" $165-225
20-24" $235-300

S & H 1249
32" tall
(Helen Teske)

Bruno Schmidt

MAKER: Bruno Schmidt of Waltershausen, Thüringia, Germany
DATE: 1900 - on
MATERIAL: Bisque head, composition body
SIZE: Various
MARK: B S W and numbers

Marked B.S.W. Character Baby: Bisque head, open mouth, sleep eyes, good wig, composition bent-limb baby body; dressed; all in good condition.

12-14"	$150-225
18-21"	$250-300

Marked B.S.W. Child Doll: Bisque head, open mouth, sleep eyes, good wig, jointed composition child body, dressed; all in good condition.

24"	$225-250

B.S.W. Tommy Tucker Character (molded and painted hair):

22-25"	$750-850

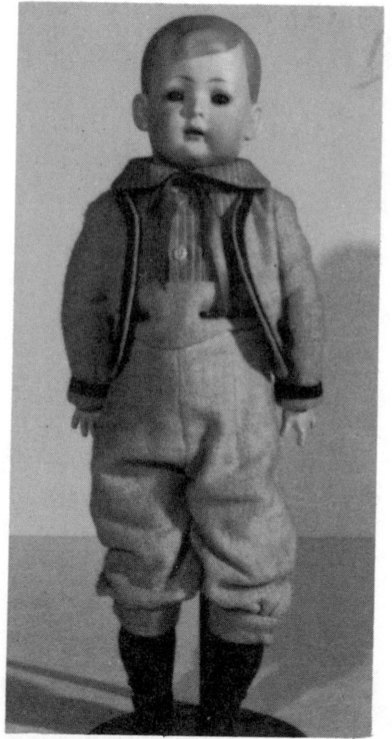

Bruno Schmidt
(So-called Tommy Tucker)
15" tall
(Clendenien Collection)

Franz Schmidt Baby or Toddler

MAKER: Franz Schmidt & Co. of Georgenthal near Waltershausen, Thüringia, Germany

DATE: Ca. 1911

MATERIAL: Bisque socket head, jointed bent-limb or toddler body of composition

SIZE: Various

MARK: "F.S. & CO." "Made in Germany." Numbers such as 1295, 1272. Deponiert included.

1295
F. S. & Co.
Made in
Germany
30

Marked F. Schmidt Doll: Bisque head, may have open nostrils, sleep eyes, open mouth, good wig; jointed bent-limb body; suitably dressed, all in good condition.

#1295	12-14"	$200-250*
	19-24"	$300-400*
Solid dome	14-16"	$300-400

*Allow extra for toddler body and and/or flirty eyes

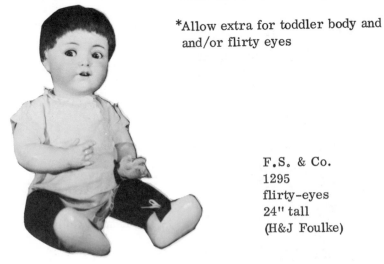

F.S. & Co.
1295
flirty-eyes
24" tall
(H&J Foulke)

Schmitt Bébé

MAKER: Schmitt & Fils, Paris, France
DATE: Ca. 1879 - 1891
MATERIAL: Bisque socket head, composition jointed body
SIZE: Various
MARK:

Marked Schmitt Bébé: Bisque socket head with closed mouth, large paperweight eyes, skin or good wig, pierced ears; Schmitt jointed composition body. Appropriate clothes. All in good condition. 15-18" $1800-2300

Schmitt
18" tall
(Joyce
Alderson)

Schoenau & Hoffmeister Character Baby

MAKER: Schoenau & Hoffmeister of Burggrub, Bavaria, Germany
DATE: 1910 - on
MATERIAL: Bisque head, composition bent-limb baby body
SIZE: Various
MARK: "Porzellanfabrik Burggrub" or , and numbers, such as 169, 769. Also "Hanna" or "Burggrub/Baby"

Marked Schoenau & Hoffmeister Baby: Bisque socket head, open mouth, good wig, sleep eyes, composition bent-limb baby body; all in good condition.

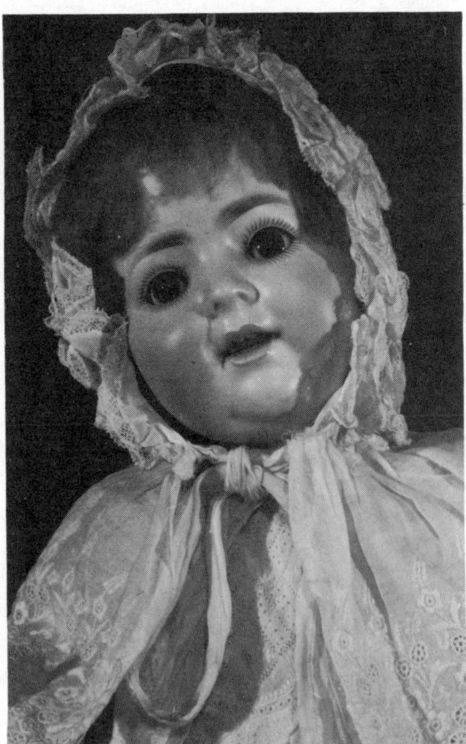

Size 12-16" $200-250
Size 22-24" $300-350

"Porzellanfabrik
Burggrub
169"
24" tall
(H & J Foulke)

Schoenau & Hoffmeister Child

MAKER: Schoenau & Hoffmeister of Burggrub, Bavaria, Germany
DATE: 1901 - on
MATERIAL: Bisque head, composition ball-jointed body
SIZE: Various
MARK: 5500 and "Porzellanfabrik Burggrub" on head, and numbers such as 1909, 5500, 5700

PB
S H
dep

Schoenau & Hoffmeister Child, Bisque head, ball-jointed body, open mouth, sleep eyes, original or good wig, original or good clothes; all in nice condition.

16-19" $150-175
24-26" $175-200

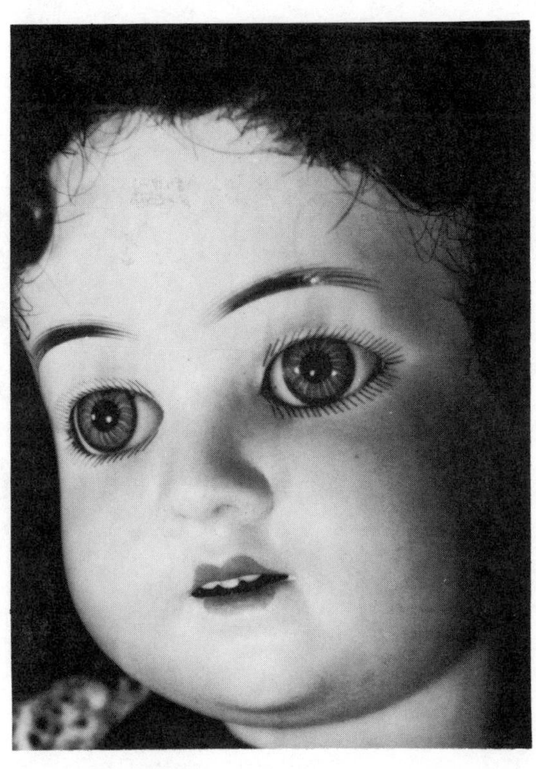

PB
S H
5500

Made in Germany
22" tall
(H & J Foulke)

Schoenhut "Baby Face"

MAKER: Albert Schoenhut & Co., Philadelphia, Penn., U.S.A.
DATE: 1913 - 1930
MATERIAL: Wood, fully jointed toddler or bent-limb baby bodies
SIZE: 13" - 17"
DESIGNER: Harry E. Schoenhut
MARK: H E Schoenhut ©1913 in a circle

Schoenhut Baby Face: Wooden head and fully jointed toddler or bent-limb baby body, marked head and/or body. Painted hair, painted eyes, open/closed mouth, suitably dressed, nothing repainted, all in good condition.

Baby body	13-15"	$250-300*
Toddler body	13-17"	$225-275*

*Allow extra for sleep eyes and open mouth.

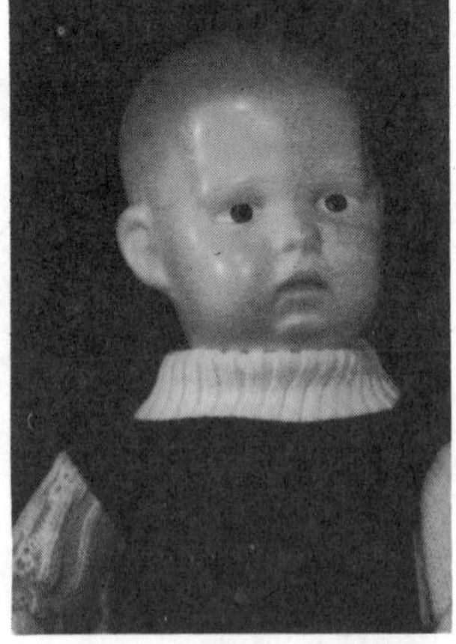

Schoenhut
"Baby Face"
Round decal mark
17" tall
(Roberta Roberts)

Schoenhut Character

MAKER: Albert Schoenhut & Co., Philadelphia, Penn., U.S.A.
DATE: 1911 to ca. 1930
MATERIAL: Wood, spring jointed
SIZE: 14" - 21"
DESIGNER: Early - Adolph Graziana; and Mr. Leslie
Later - Harry E. Schoenhut
MARK: SCHOENHUT DOLL PAT. Jan. 17TH 1911 U. S. A.

SCHOENHUT DOLL
PAT. JAN. 17, '11, U.S.A.
& FOREIGN COUNTRIES

Schoenhut Character Doll: Wooden head and spring-jointed wooden body, marked head and/or body, original wig, brown or blue intaglio eyes, open/closed mouth with painted teeth, or closed mouth; original or suitable clothing, nothing repainted; all in good condition.

Size 16-19" $350 up

Schoenhut Pouty Character
16" tall
Impressed mark
(Roberta Roberts)

Schoenhut Character
(Molded Hair)

MAKER: Albert Schoenhut & Co., Philadelphia, Penn. U.S.A.
DATE: 1911-1930
MATERIAL: All wood
SIZE: 14" - 21"
MARK:

SCHOENHUT DOLL
PAT. JAN. 17,'11, U.S.A.
& FOREIGN COUNTRIES

Schoenhut "Molded Hair": Wooden head with molded hair, comb marks, possibly a ribbon or bow, intaglio eyes, mouth usually closed; spring-jointed wood body; original or suitable clothes; all in good condition. 14-16" $450 up

"Molded Hair"
Schoenhut
With pink ribbon
17" tall
(Roberta Roberts)

Schoenhut "Doll Face"

MAKER: Albert Schoenhut & Co., Philadelphia, Penn., U.S.A.
DATE: 1915 - 1930
MATERIAL: All wood
SIZE: 14" - 21"
MARK:

SCHOENHUT DOLL
PAT. JAN. 17,'11, U.S.A.
& FOREIGN COUNTRIES

Schoenhut "Doll Face": Wooden head and spring-jointed wooden body, original mohair wig, decal eyes, open/closed mouth with painted teeth; original or suitable clothes; all in good condition.

Size 14-16" $275-300
Size 19-21" $300-325

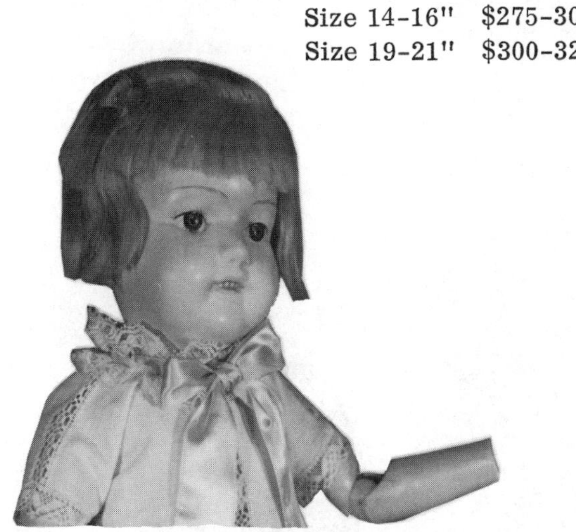

Schoenhut
"Doll Face"
21" tall
Oval decal mark
All original
(Roberta Roberts)

Schoenhut Rolly Dolly

MAKER: Schoenhut Co., Philadelphia, Penn., U.S.A.
DATE: 1902 - on
MATERIAL: All papier-mâché, weighted bottom
SIZE: Various
MARK: "Schoenhut Rolly Dolly" on label

Marked "Rolly Dolly": All papier-mâché, molded and painted hair, hat and features. Egg-shaped body with molded and painted clothes. In good condition. Large $150 up*
Small $75 up*

* Not enough price samples to justify a reliable range.

*These prices are for <u>Schoenhut</u> only; other Rolly Dolly toys much less

Unmarked
Rolly Dolly
(Joyce Alderson)

Schoenhut Walker

MAKER: Albert Schoenhut & Co., Philadelphia, Penn., U.S.A.
DATE: 1919 - 1930
MATERIAL: All wood
SIZE: 11" - 17"
MARK:

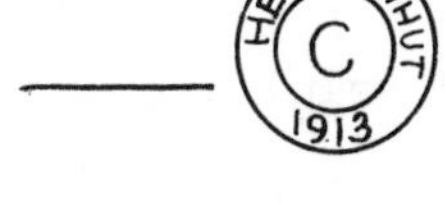

Schoenhut Walker: All wood with "infant type" head, mohair wig, painted eyes, curved arms, straight legs with "walker" joint at hip; original or appropriate clothes; all in good condition.

Size 11-13" $250-300

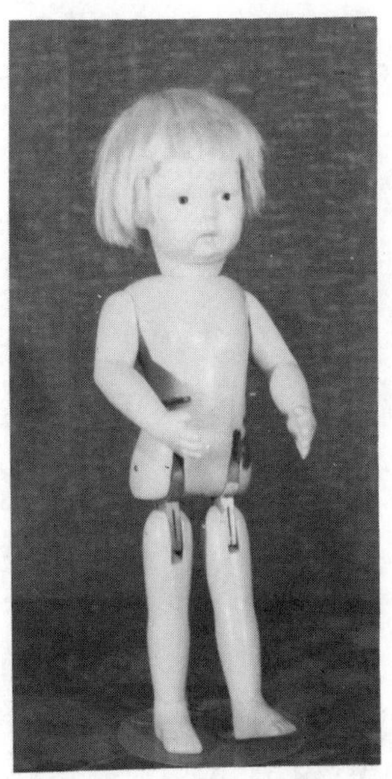

Schoenhut Walker
14" tall
(Roberta Roberts)

Scootles

MAKER: Cameo Doll Products Co. Inc., Port Allegany, Penn., U.S.A.
DATE: Ca. 1925 - on
MATERIAL: All composition or all bisque
SIZE: Many
DESIGNER: Rose O'Neill
MARK: All Bisque: "Scootles" on red and gold chest label; "Germany" and "Rose O'Neill" on feet
Composition: SCOOTLES

Scootles: Marked, all composition, jointed at neck, shoulders and hips, blue or brown painted eyes, closed smiling mouth, molded hair, eyes to side, not dressed; doll in nice condition.
Size 12" $150-175

All bisque jointed at shoulders only, molded hair and painted features. Size 6-1/2" $225 up

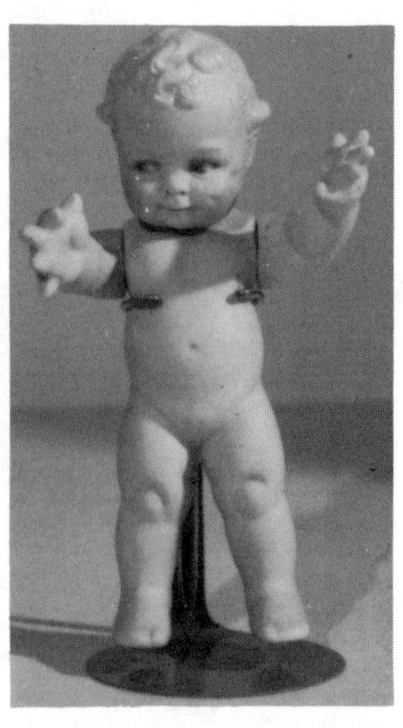

Left: Scootles, all composition, 12" tall (Clendenien Collection)
Right: Scootles, all bisque, 6-1/2" tall (Clendenien Collection)

Anne Shirley

(EFFanBEE)

MAKER: EFFanBEE Doll Corp. (Fleischaker & Baum), New York, N. Y., U.S.A.
DATE: 1935 to ca. 1948
MATERIAL: Composition
SIZE: Various
MARK: Raised letters on back. Caution - "Anne Shirley" body was used with many different heads.

EFFANBEE
ANNE SHIRLEY

Marked Anne Shirley: All composition, jointed neck, shoulders, and hips; sleep eyes, closed mouth, original human hair wig and clothes, good condition.

15"	$60-70
18"	$65-85
20-21"	$100-125

"Anne Shirley"
21" tall
(Emily Manning)

Simon & Halbig

(#1160)

MAKER: Simon & Halbig of Gräfenhain, Thüringia, Germany
DATE: Ca. 1900
MATERIAL: Bisque head, cloth body with bisque limbs
SIZE: Various, usually small
MARK: "S & H 1160"

S & H
1160 - 2/0

Marked S & H 1160 (So-called Little Women type): Shoulder head with closed mouth, glass set eyes, fancy mohair wig; cloth body with bisque limbs, molded boots; dressed; all in good condition.

6-7"	$150-185
8-10"	$200-250
13"	$400

S & H
1160
5 1/2" tall
(Helen Teske)

Simon & Halbig
(Kid Body)

MAKER: Simon and Halbig of Gräfenhain, Thüringia, Germany
DATE: Ca. 1880's to ca. 1930's
MATERIAL: Bisque shoulder head, kid or kid and cloth body
SIZE: Various
MARK: "S & H" and/or "Simon & Halbig" with numbers such as 1010, 1040, 1080, 1250, 950 and often "DEP" and/or "Germany"

S & H Shoulder Head: Marked bisque shoulder head, kid body, bisque arms with cloth legs, open mouth, sleep eyes, pierced ears, well costumed; all in nice condition.

#1009, swivel neck, fashion body:	20-22"	$295-325
#1040, 1080, 1250:	16-20"	$175-200
	21-25"	$200-250

"S & H 1040"
Shoulder head
19" tall
(H & J Foulke)

Simon & Halbig Character Baby

MAKER: Simon & Halbig of Gräfenhain, Thüringia, Germany
DATE: 1909 - on
MATERIAL: Bisque head, bent-limb composition body
SIZE: Various
MARK: "Simon & Halbig" and "Germany" and numbers such as 1294, 1488, 1498

Marked S & H Baby: Bisque head, short curly wig of mohair, open mouth, sleep eyes with lashes, composition bent-limb baby body; nicely dressed; all in very good condition.

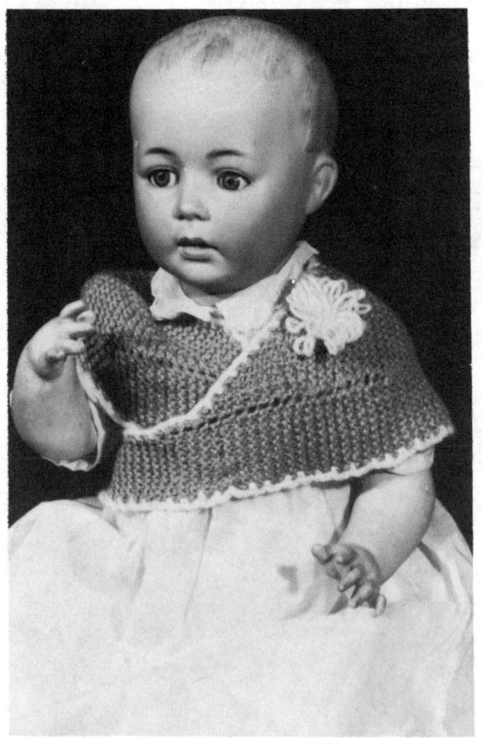

#1294: 16-22" $350-400
#1388, 1488,
1498: $500 up

Rare
"1498"
19" tall
(Richard Wright)

Simon & Halbig Child
(Closed Mouth)

MAKER: Simon & Halbig of Gräfenhain, Thüringia, Germany
DATE: Ca. 1880's
MATERIAL: Bisque socket head on ball-jointed wood and composition body or shoulder head on jointed kid body with bisque lower arms
SIZE: Various
MARK: "S & H" or "Simon & Halbig" with numbers, such as 949, 950, 939, etc.

S 13 H
949

Marked S & H Child: Bisque head, glass eyes, closed mouth, pierced ears, good wig, dressed; body as above in good condition.

15-16"	$450-500
21-23"	$550-650
27-28"	$800-850

S & H
950
Shoulder head
10 1/2" tall
(H&J Foulke)

Simon & Halbig Child
(Composition Body)

MAKER: Simon and Halbig of Gräfenhain, Thüringia, Germany
DATE: At least from 1889 into the 1930's
MATERIAL: Bisque head, composition ball-jointed body; sometimes French type, part wood
SIZE: Various
MARK: "S & H" and/or "Simon & Halbig" with numbers, such as 1079, 1039, 550, 1009, and often "DEP" and/or "Germany"

1079-2
DEP
S H
Germany

Marked S & H Child: Bisque head, good wig, original ball-jointed composition body; sleep eyes, open mouth, pierced ears; very pretty clothes; all in nice condition.

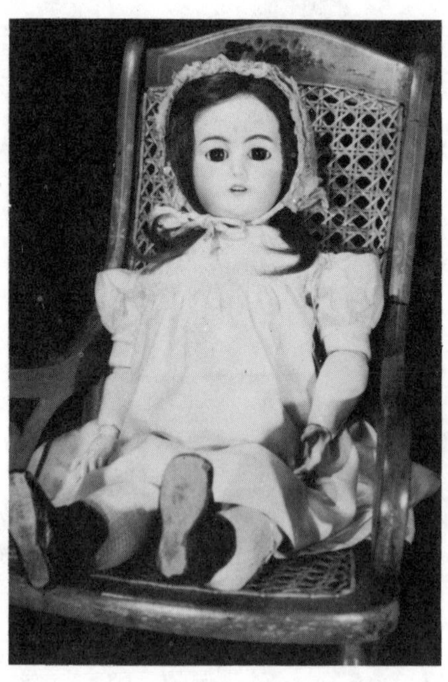

#949: 18-23" $275-350

#1079, 550, & other common molds:

15-17"	$185*
21-25"	$200-250*
28-30"	$300-325*
31-33"	$325-350*

*Allow extra for #1279, #1249, #1299 and flirty-eyes or walkers

1079
S & H
Germany
26" tall
(H&J Foulke)

Simon & Halbig Lady Doll

MAKER: Simon & Halbig of Gräfenhain, Thüringia, Germany
DATE: Ca. 1910
MATERIAL: Bisque socket head, composition lady body, molded bust, slim-type arms and legs
SIZE: Various
MARK: "S & H"

Marked S & H 1159 Lady Doll: Bisque socket head, open mouth, good wig, pierced ears, sleep eyes, lady body as above, elegantly dressed; all in good condition. Size 20-22" $500-700

Marked S & H Lady with closed mouth: Bisque head with set glass eyes, good wig, composition lady body as above; nicely dressed; all in good condition. Size 14-15" $450-600

"Simon & Halbig" closed-mouth lady (Joyce Alderson)

Simon & Halbig Tiny Doll

MAKER: Simon and Halbig of Gräfenhain, Thüringia, Germany
DATE: Ca. 1889 into 1930's
MATERIAL: Bisque head, 5-piece composition body with painted shoes and socks
SIZE: 6" - 12"
MARK: "S&H" and/or "SIMON & HALBIG" with numbers, such as 1079 and 1078, and often "DEP" and/or "Germany"

Tiny Marked S & H: Bisque head, composition body of five pieces, open mouth, nice wig, sleep eyes, original clothes; all in good condition.

7-9"
$125-150*
*Allow extra for for a fully jointed body.

Pair of S & H 1079 Dolls 9 1/2" and 10" (H&J Foulke)

Skippy

MAKER: EFFanBEE Doll Co., (Bernard Fleischaker & Hugo Baum), New York, N.Y., U.S.A.
DATE: Ca. 1928 - on
MATERIAL: Composition
SIZE: 14 inches
DESIGNER: P. L. Crosby
MARK:

EFFANBEE
SKIPPY
©
P.L. Crosby

Skippy Marked Head: All composition (later, a cloth torso), jointed at neck, hips and shoulders; molded hair; painted eyes to side, dressed, in good condition.

14" $85-100

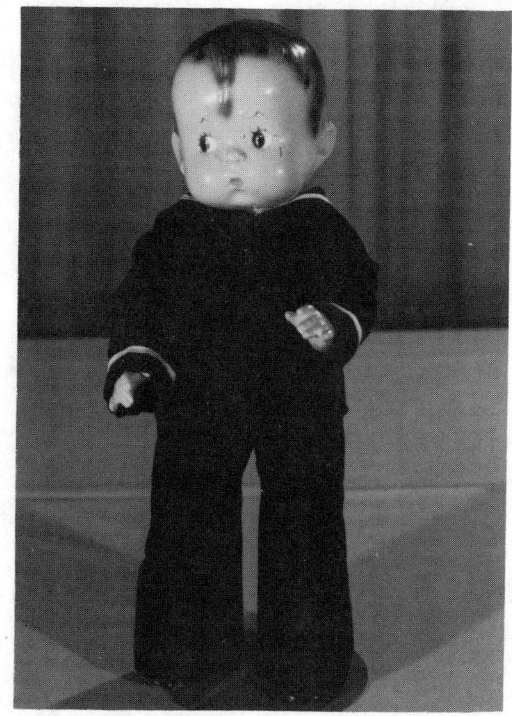

Skippy
14" tall
Redressed
(Barbara Crescenze)

Skookum Indian Doll

(McAboy)

MAKER: H.H. Tammen Co., New York, N.Y., Denver, Colo., and Los Angeles, Ca., U.S.A.
DATE: 1913 - on
MATERIAL: Composition or celluloid type mask faces; excelsior stuffed cloth bodies; wooden legs, composition feet
SIZE: 3" to 42"
DESIGNER and ORIGINATOR: Mary McAboy, Denver, Colo.
MARK: Sometimes marked "SKOOKUMS" on sole of foot

SKOOKUM Indian Doll: Indian blanket clad doll - folds in blanket represent arms; mask face, cotton print dress or cotton shirt and felt trousers, eyes to side, black hair, head band with one or more feathers; beads etc., all very colorful, in good condition.

Size 10-12" $45-50

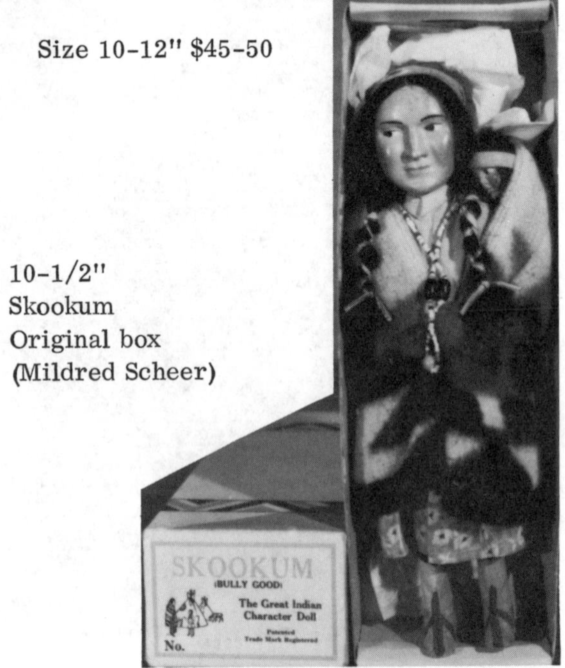

10-1/2"
Skookum
Original box
(Mildred Scheer)

Snow Babies

MAKER: Various German firms
DATE: 1920 - 1930
MATERIAL: All bisque
SIZE: 1 - 3" usually
MARK: Sometimes "Germany"

Snow Babies: All bisque with snow suits and caps of pebbly-textured bisque. Painted features. Various standing, lying or sitting positions. $22 and up depending upon action and accessories

Snow Babies
1-1 1/2" high
(H&J Foulke)

Snow White

MAKER: Ideal Novelty & Toy Co., New York, N.Y., U.S.A.
DATE: Ca. 1939
MATERIAL: All composition
SIZE: 18 inches
MARK: On body - SHIRLEY TEMPLE/18
On dress - "An Ideal Doll"

Snow White: All composition jointed at neck, shoulders and hips. Black mohair wig, lashed sleeping eyes, open mouth. Original dress with velvet bodice and cape and rayon skirt with figures of seven dwarfs. In good condition. $90-100

Snow White
18"
All original
(Helen Teske)

Mae Starr

(Talking Doll)

MAKER: EFFanBEE Doll Co., New York, N.Y., U.S.A.
DATE: 1928
MATERIAL: Composition head and limbs, cloth body
SIZE: 29"
MARK:

MAE
STARR
DOLL

Mae Starr: Composition shoulder head with open mouth, sleep eyes, human hair wig, cloth body, composition limbs. Talking device in center of torso with records.
29" $150-185

(See Anderton, Twentieth Century Dolls, p. 433, illustration W-T-9)

Steiff Dolls

MAKER: Fraülein Margarete Steiff, Würtemberg, Germany
DATE: 1894 - on
MATERIAL: Felt, plush, or velvet
SIZE: Various
MARK: Metal button in ear

Steiff Doll: Felt, plush or velvet, jointed. Seam down middle of face, button eyes, painted features, original clothes. Most are character dolls. Many have large shoes to enable them to stand. All in good condition.

Size 10-15" $100-135

11" tall
Original clothes
(Joyce Alderson)

Herm Steiner

MAKER: Hermann Steiner of Sonneberg, Thüringia, Germany
DATE: 1920's
MATERIAL: Bisque head, cloth or composition body
SIZE: Various, usually small
MARK:

15 HS Germany 240

Herm Steiner HS Germany

Herm Steiner Baby: Bisque head, cloth body, molded hair, sleep eyes, dressed; in good condition. 6-10" $100-150*

Herm Steiner Child Doll: Bisque head, jointed composition body, wig, sleeping eyes, open mouth, dressed; in good condition. Size 12-14" $110-135

*Allow extra for character face.

HS

9-1/2" long
Unusual character
(Joyce Alderson)

Jules Steiner Bébé

MAKER: Jules Nicholas Steiner (and successors), Paris, France
DATE: 1870's to ca. 1908
MATERIAL: Bisque head, jointed papier-mâché body
SIZE: Various
MARK: (In part) "LE PARISIEN--PARIS", "BÉBÉ LE PARISIEN", "BÉBÉ STEINER", "STEINER S.G.D.G."

Steiner Bébé: Marked bisque head, jointed papier-mâché body, good French wig, closed mouth, beautiful paperweight eyes, lovely clothes, all in good condition.

8-10" $850-900
16-18" $900-1000
21-23" $1000-1250

Open mouth, two rows of teeth:
17-21" $700-850

Open mouth:
20-22" $500-550

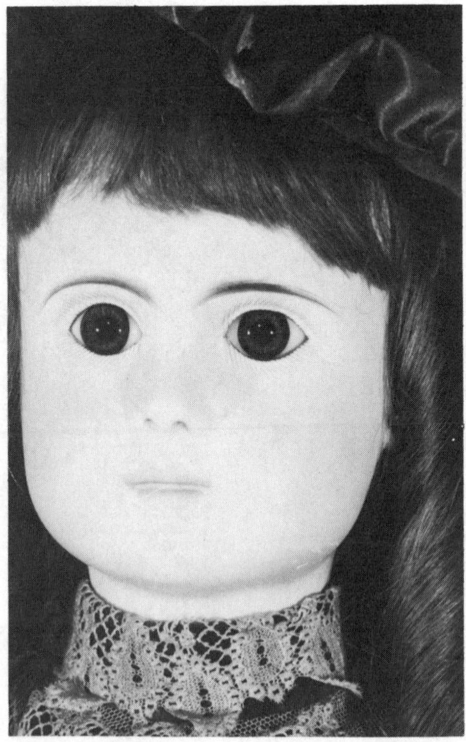

A-19
Paris
Le Parisien
29" tall
(Jan Foulke)

Superior Dolls

MAKER: Unknown German firms
DATE: Ca. 1870 - on
MATERIAL: Composition head, cloth body, cloth or kid extremities
SIZE: Various
MARK: Label "M & S SUPERIOR 2015" or G.L. 2015 SUPERIOR PERFECTLY HARMLESS" or "M & S SUPERIOR 4515," etc. Later ones also marked "Germany"

Superior Doll: Label on back of shoulder head; papier-mâché shoulder head, black or blond molded painted hair; original cloth body, old kid arms and boots, quaint old clothing, brown or blue painted eyes; all in nice condition.

14-21"	$165-235
28"	$250-300

Unmarked Superior - type 22" tall (Helen Teske)

Suzette

MAKER: EFFanBEE Doll Corporation (Fleischaker & Baum), New York, N.Y., U.S.A.
DATE: 1939
MATERIAL: All composition
SIZE: 11 inches
MARK:

SUZETTE
EFF AN BEE
MADE IN
U.S.A.

Marked Suzette: All composition jointed neck, shoulders and hips, closed mouth, eyes painted to side, mohair wig, original clothes; all in good condition. 11-1/2" $50-60

Marked Suzanne, a sister doll of the same period, with sleeping eyes. 14" $45-55

Suzette
11"
All original
(H & J Foulke)

Shirley Temple
(Ideal)

MAKER: Ideal Toy Corp., New York, N.Y., U.S.A.
DATE: 1934 - on
MATERIAL: Composition, jointed at neck, shoulders and hips
SIZE: 11" to 27"
DESIGNER: Bernard Lipfert
MARK: "SHIRLEY TEMPLE --IDEAL" on head and torso

Marked Shirley Temple: Marked head and body, jointed composition body, all original including wig and clothes. Entire doll in good condition.

Size 11" $175-200
Size 13" $125-140
Size 18" $165-200
Size 27" $300-350

"Shirley Temple"
All original
11" tall
(H & J Foulke)

Shirley Temple

(Vinyl)

MAKER: Ideal Toy Corporation, New York, N.Y., U.S.A.
DATE: 1957
MATERIAL: Vinyl and plastic
SIZE: 12" - 19"
MARK: "Ideal Doll"
"ST-12" (number denotes size)

Ideal Shirley Temple: Vinyl and plastic, rooted hair, sleep eyes, jointed at shoulders and hips, original clothes; all in good condition.

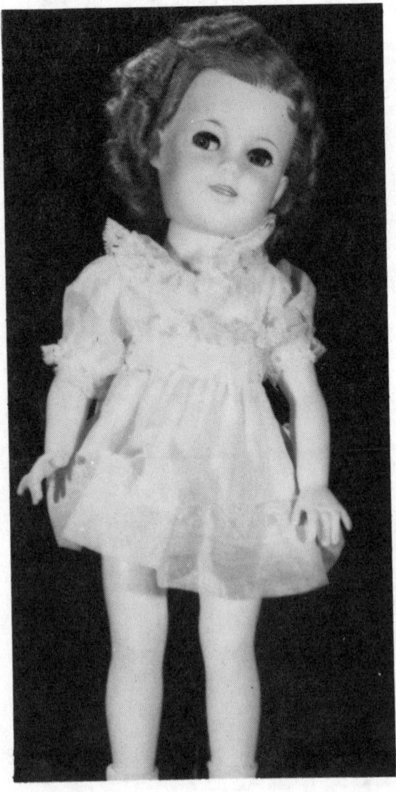

12"	$25-35
17-19"	$50-60

Vinyl Shirley Temple
18" tall
All original
(Emily Manning)

Shirley Temple Baby

MAKER: Ideal Novelty & Toy Co., New York, N.Y., U.S.A.
DATE: 1934
MATERIAL: Composition swivel head on shoulder plate, arms and legs; soft cloth body
SIZE: 16" to 25" in six sizes
MARK: SHIRLEY TEMPLE on head

Marked Shirley Baby: Composition swivel head with sleeping eyes, open smiling mouth, dimples, molded hair or blond mohair wig; cloth body, composition arms and legs. Appropriate clothes. All in good condition

16-20" $225-250+

*A very hard to find doll.

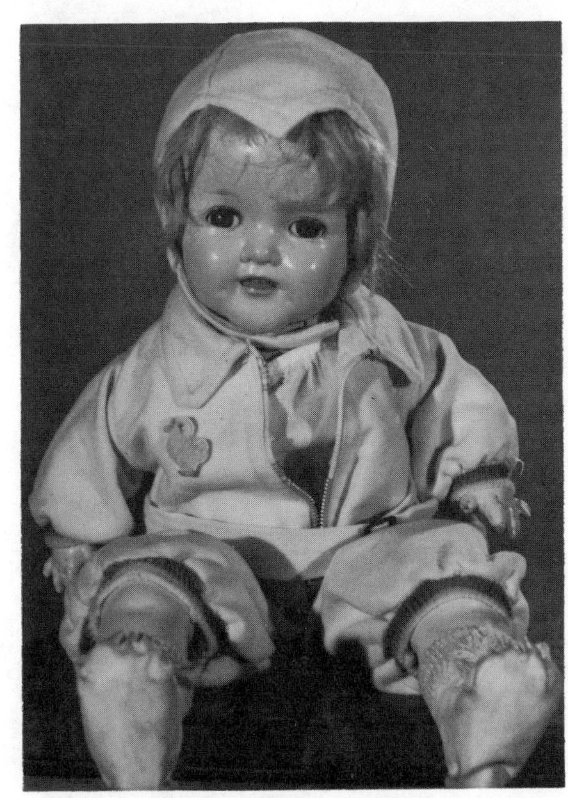

16" Baby Shirley Original labeled clothes (Helen Teske)

Three-Faced Doll

MAKER: Perhaps Carl Bergner of Sonneberg, Thüringia, Germany
DATE: Early 20th Century
MATERIAL: Bisque head with three faces, cloth torso, composition arms & cap
SIZE: Smaller, such as 11" and 13"
MARK: "C. B." on back shoulder

MARKED:"C. B." Multi-face: Bisque head with three different faces (usually sleeping, laughing and crying). Dressed. All in good condition.

11-13" $1000-1300

Multi-face doll
Marked "C. B."
12" tall
(Emma Wedmore)

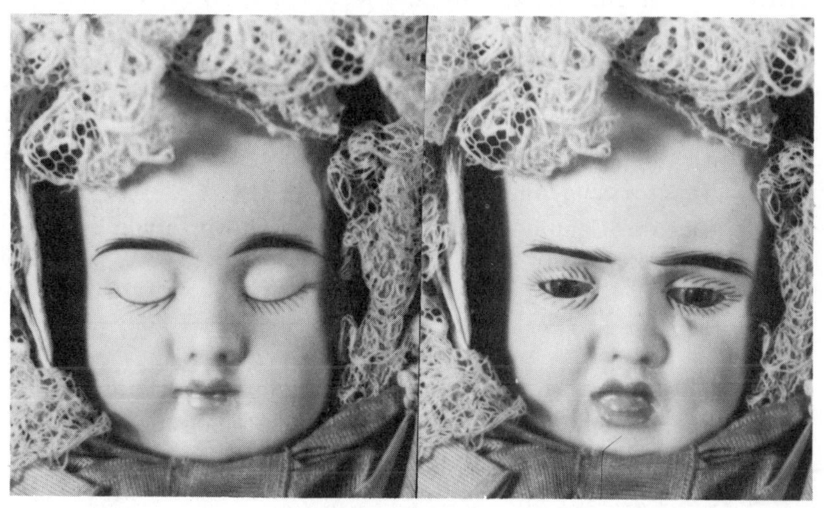

Multiface Doll
marked "C.B"
12" tall.
The close-up
pictures show the
different faces.
(Emma Wedmore)

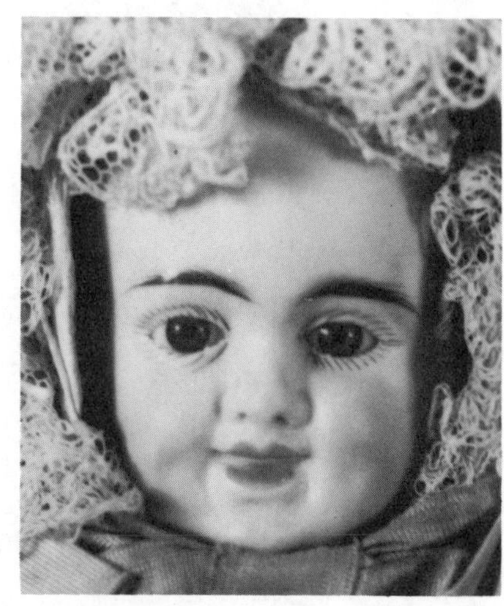

Toni

MAKER: Ideal Novelty & Toy Co., New York, N.Y., U.S.A.
DATE: 1948 - on
MATERIAL: Hard plastic, swivel neck, jointed shoulders and hips
SIZE: 14 to 21 inches
DESIGNER: Bernard Lipfert
MARK: Head: P-90/Ideal Doll/Made in U.S.A.
Dress: Genuine Toni Doll/with Nylon wig/Made by Ideal Novelty & Toy

---

Marked Toni Doll: All hard plastic, jointed neck, shoulders and hips, sleeping eyes, nylon wig, closed mouth. Original clothes. Excellent condition.

14-15"	$30-35*
21"	$40*

*Allow extra for a walker

Toni
14" tall
All original except footwear
(H&J Foulke)

Toto

MAKER: Lanternier, Limoges, France
DATE: Ca. 1915 - 1925
MATERIAL: Bisque head, jointed composition body
SIZE: Various
MARK: "Toto, AL & C, Limoges"

Marked Toto: Bisque character face with smiling face, open-closed mouth with molded teeth, glass eyes, pierced ears, good wig, jointed French composition body; dressed; all in good condition. 18-23" $425-575

Trilby

MAKER: American Stuffed Novelty Co., New York, N.Y., U.S.A.
DATE: Ca. 1924
MATERIAL: All cloth
SIZE: 11", 16", 19"
MARK: None

Trilby: All cloth with painted features, mohair wig, jointed shoulders and hips. Original clothes. All in good condition.

Size 16" $100-125*

*Not enough price samples to justify a reliable range.

Trilby
11" tall
(Clendenien Collection)

Trudy

(Three-faced Doll)

MAKER: Three-in-One Doll Corporation, New York, N.Y., U.S.A.
DATE: 1946
MATERIAL: Composition head, arms and legs; cloth body
SIZE: Various
MARK: On clothing (see below)

Trudy, Three-faced Doll: Composition head, arms and legs, cloth body, composition knob on top of head which turns faces, original dress and bonnet marked: "Sleepy Trudy, Smily Trudy, Weepy Trudy" in tiny pastel circles printed on white dress material. All fine condition. 16" $75-85

Unmarked Trudy
Showing smiling face
All original
14" tall
(H&J Foulke)

Tommy Tucker*

MAKER: EFFanBEE Doll Corporation (Fleischaker & Baum), New York, N.Y., U.S.A.
DATE: 1939 - 1949
MATERIAL: Composition head and hands; stuffed body; or all composition
SIZE: 15" - 24"
MARK: **EFFANBEE**
U.S.A.

Tommy Tucker, Mickey, and Baby Bright Eyes: Composition head with painted hair or mohair wig, closed mouth, chubby cheeks, flirting eyes; body as above; original clothes; all in good condition. 18" $75-85

*Also called "Mickey" and "Baby Bright Eyes"

Tagged "Tommy Tucker" 17" tall (H&J Foulke)

Tynie Baby

MAKER: E.I. Horsman Co., New York, N.Y., U.S.A.
DATE: 1924
MATERIAL: Bisque head, cloth body, composition arms; also, composition head and all bisque versions were made
SIZE: Various
DESIGNER: Bernard Lipfert
MARK:

© 1924
E.I. Horsman Inc.
Made in
Germany

Marked Tynie Baby: Bisque solid infant head with sleeping eyes, closed mouth, slightly frowning face, cloth body with composition arms. Appropriate clothes. All in good condition.

12-13" $350
All bisque with swivel neck, glass eyes: 9" $450-500*
Composition head: 13" $50-60*

*Not enough price samples to justify a reliable range.

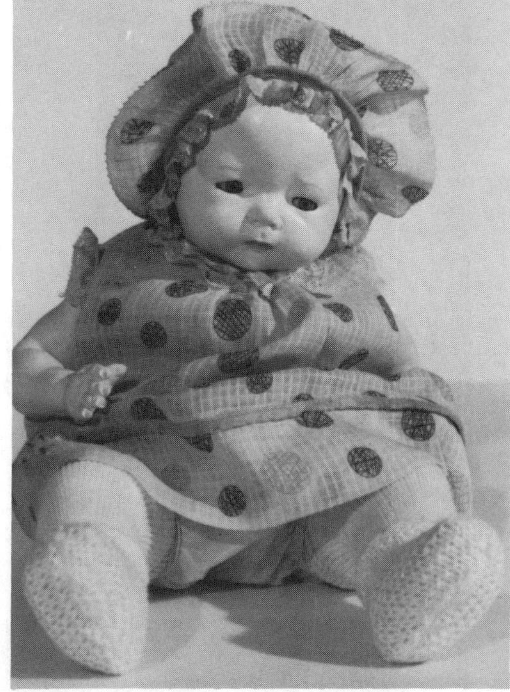

Composition head Tynie Baby 15" tall (Clendenien Collection)

Uneeda Biscuit Boy

MAKER: Ideal Novelty & Toy Co., New York, N.Y., U.S.A.
DATE: Ca. 1914 - 1919
MATERIAL: Composition head, arms and legs; cloth body
SIZE: 16 inches
MARK: Label on sleeve "Uneeda Kid/Patented Dec 8, 1914/ Ideal Novelty & Toy Co./Brooklyn, N.Y."

Biscuit Boy: Composition head with molded brown hair, painted blue eyes, closed mouth. Cloth body with composition arms and legs. Wearing molded black boots, bloomer suit, yellow slicker, and rainhat, and carrying a box of Uneeda Biscuits. All in good condition, showing some wear.

Size 16" $85-95

Uneeda Kid
16" tall
(Joyce Alderson)

Unis Child Doll

MAKER: Société Française de Fabrication de Bébés et Jouets. (S.F.B.J.) of Paris and Montruil-sous-Bois, France

DATE: 1922 - on

MATERIAL: Bisque head, jointed papier-mâché body

SIZE: Various

MARK: 71 UNIS FRANCE 149 301 Also "Unis France 71 149 301" "71 Unis France 149 60"

Unis Child Doll: Marked bisque head, papier-mâché body or wood and papier-mâché jointed body; sleep eyes, good wig, pretty clothes, pierced ears, open mouth; all in nice condition. Size 20-24" $250-300

Unis 301
12"
All original
(Becky Roberts)

Unis Costume Doll

MAKER: Société Française de Fabrication de Bébés et Jouets, Paris, France
DATE: 1922 - on
MATERIAL: Bisque head, papier-mâché body
SIZE: Usually 12" or under
MARK:

71 UNIS FRANCE 149
301

Unis Costume Doll: Marked bisque head, sleep eyes, mohair wig, open or closed mouth; papier-mâché body; original costume. All in good condition. 5-7" $85-125

Dark skinned:
11-13" $135-165

Unis
301
5" tall
All original
(H & J Foulke)

Vanta Baby

MAKER: Louis Amberg & Sons, New York, N.Y., U.S.A.
DATE: 1927
MATERIAL: Composition shoulder head, arms and legs; muslin torso
SIZE: Several
MARK: "VANTA BABY-AMBERG" embossed on torso

Marked Vanta Baby: Composition shoulder head, molded and painted hair, metal sleeping eyes, open closed mouth with two teeth; curved composition arms and legs, muslin body, jointed hips and shoulders, suitably dressed. All in good condition. Size 24" $50-65

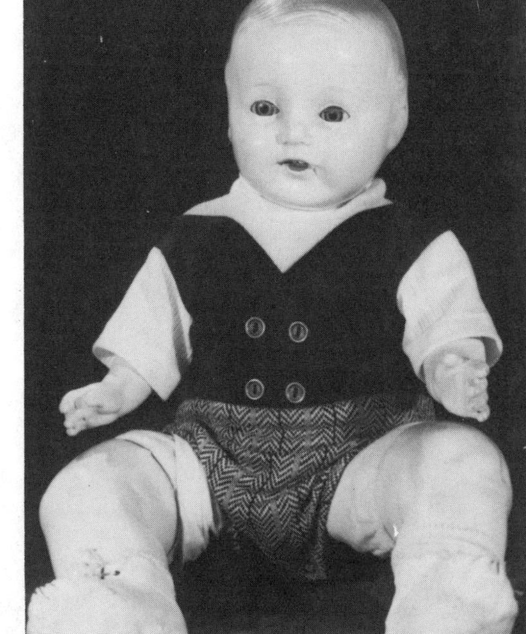

Vanta Baby
22" tall
(Emily Manning)

Izannah Walker

MAKER: Izannah Walker, Central Falls, R.I., U.S.A.
DATE: 1873
MATERIAL: All cloth
SIZE: 15" - 24"
MARK: *Patented Nov. 4th 1873*

Izannah Walker Doll: Stockinette, pressed head, features and hair painted with oils, applied ears, treated limbs, muslin body, appropriate clothes. In fair condition.

Size 20-24" $975

For photo see, COLLECTOR'S ENCYCLOPEDIA OF DOLLS, the Colemans, p. 634 & 635.

Jeannie Walker

MAKER: Alexander Doll Co., New York, N.Y., U.S.A.
DATE: 1942
MATERIAL: All composition
SIZE: 13" - 19"
MARK: Body - "Alexander Pat. No. 2171281"
Dress tag - "Jeannie Walker-Madame Alexander-N.Y., U.S.A. All rights reserved"

Marked "Jeannie Walker": All composition with walking mechanism; sleep eyes, closed mouth, human hair or mohair wig, dressed; all in good condition.

Size 13-18" $90-125

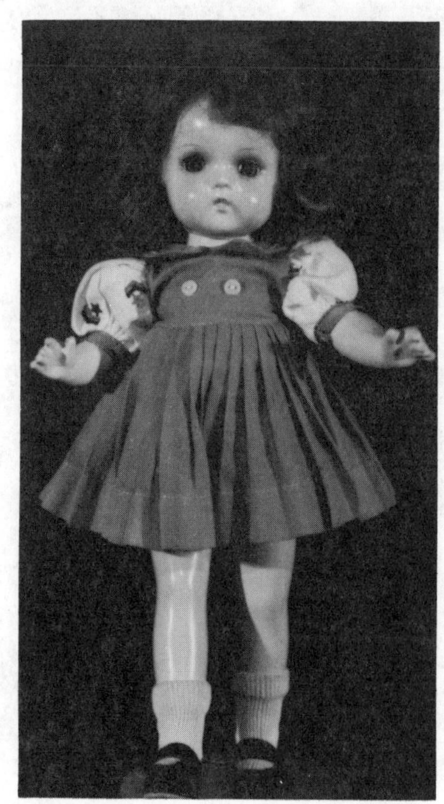

Alexander
Jeannie Walker
All original
14" tall
(Jan Foulke)

Walküre Child Doll

MAKER: Kley and Hahn of Ohrdruf, Thüringia, Germany
DATE: Ca. 1902 - on
MATERIAL: Bisque head, composition ball-jointed body
SIZE: Various
MARK: "Walküre - K & H Germany" etc.

K H
Walküre

Walküre Doll: Marked bisque head, ball-jointed composition body, good wig, open mouth, pierced ears, blue or brown sleep eyes; well dressed, all in nice condition.

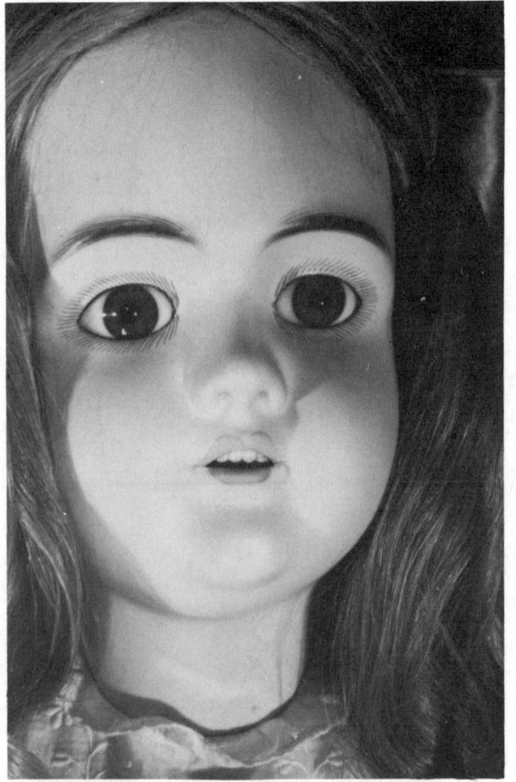

28-30" $275-300
33-34" $375-400

Walküre
Germany
34" tall
(H & J Foulke)

Wax Doll-Poured
(Montanari or Pierotti-type)

MAKER: Various firms in England
DATE: Mid-19th century through the early 1900's
MATERIAL: Wax head, arms and legs; cloth body
SIZE: Various
MARK: None

Unmarked Poured Wax Doll: Head, lower arms and legs of wax; cloth body, blue or brown glass eyes, blond or brown set-in hair; original clothes or very well dressed; all in good condition. 19-24" $525-600*

*Allow extra for signed Pierotti, Montanari or Mrs. Peck.

Same as above with wig instead of inset hair: 20-26" $250-325

Fashion-type body: 14-18" $300-400

24" Pierotti type
Poured wax
All original
(Emily Manning)

Wax Over Composition

MAKER: Numerous firms in England, Germany, or France
DATE: During the 1800's
MATERIAL: Wax over shoulder head of some type of composition or papier-mâché; cloth body; wax over composition or wooden limbs
SIZE: Various
MARK: None

Bonnet Wax Doll: Ca. 1860 to 1880: Wax over shoulder head, original cloth body and wooden extremities; blue, brown or black set eyes; nice old clothes. All in good condition.

Size 20" $225*

*Not enough price samples to justify a reliable range.

Pumpkin Head Doll: Ca. 1850 to 1890: Wax over shoulder head, molded band in molded blond hair pompadour, original cloth body, black, blue or brown glass sleep or set eyes; wax over or wooden extremities with molded socks or boots, nice old clothes, not rewaxed. All in good condition.

Size 20-22" $200-225
Size 26" $250-300

Wax Doll with wig: Ca. mid-19th century into early twentieth century: Wax over shoulder head, not rewaxed, original cloth body, blond or brown human hair or mohair wig; blue, brown or black glass eyes, sleep or set; open or closed mouth, any combination of extremities mentioned above; also arms may be made of china. Original clothing or suitably dressed; entire doll in nice condition.

Size 19-22" $200-225
Size 24-27" $250-300

English Slit-head Wax: Ca. 1830-1860; Wax over shoulder head, not rewaxed, original cloth body with leather arms; human hair wig, glass eyes (may open and close by a wire); faintly smiling. Original or suitable old clothing. All in good condition.

Size 25-27" $250-300

Top Left: Pumpkin head
15" tall
(Emily Manning)

Top right: 25" tall
Wax doll with
human hair wig
and glass eyes.
(Emily Manning)

Bottom right: 28" tall
English Wax
(Emily Manning)

Norah Wellings

MAKER: Victoria Toy Works, Wellington, Shropshire, England, for Norah Wellings
DATE: 1926 to ca. 1960
MATERIAL: Fabric: felt, velvet and velour etc. Stuffed
SIZE: Various
DESIGNER: Norah Wellings
MARK: On tag on foot: "Made in England by Norah Wellings"

Wellings Doll: All fabric, stitch jointed shoulders and hips. Molded fabric face (also of papier-mâché, sometimes stockinette covered), painted features. All in excellent condition. Most commonly found are sailors, Canadian Mounties, Scots and Black Islanders.

Sailors	8-11"	$15-20
others		$20-25
Size	12-14"	$35-55

Norah Wellings
Scots Boy
10" tall
(Helen Teske)

Wendy-Ann

(Mme. Alexander)

MAKER: Alexander Doll Co. of New York, N.Y., U.S.A.
DATE: 1938
MATERIAL: All composition, jointed at waist, neck, shoulders and hips
SIZE: 13-1/2 inches
MARK: Embossed on back of body: "Wendy-Ann - Mme. Alexander - New York, N.Y."

Wendy-Ann: Composition doll, jointed as above; nicely dressed, sleep eyes, closed mouth, beautiful human hair wig; all in very good condition.

Size 13-1/2" $55-65

9" tall
Wendy-Ann
With painted eyes
(Emily Manning)

Jane Withers

MAKER: Alexander Doll Co., New York, N.Y., U.S.A.
DATE: 1936
MATERIAL: All composition
SIZE: 17" and 20"
MARK: Dress tag - Jane Withers/All Rights Reserved/ Madame Alexander, N.Y.

Jane Withers: Composition swivel head, dark mohair wig, open smiling mouth, lashed sleep eyes; jointed shoulders and hips; original clothes; all in good condition.

Size 17-20" $150* up
Closed mouth:
Size 12" $150* up

*Not enough price samples to justify a reliable range.

Rare
Closed-mouth
Jane Withers
13" tall
Original clothes
(Rosemary Dent)

Glossary

Applied ears: Ear molded independently and affixed to the head (On most dolls the ear is included as part of the head mold).

Bald head: Head with no crown opening, could be covered by a wig or have painted hair.

Ball-jointed body: Usually a body of composition with wooden balls at knees, elbows, hips, and shoulders to make swivel joints.

Belton-type: A bald head with one, two, or three small holes for attaching wig.

Bent-limb Baby Body: Composition body of five pieces with chubby torso and curved arms and legs.

Biskoline: Celluloid-type of substance for making dolls.

Breather: Doll with an actual opening in each nostril; also called open nostrils.

Breveté (or Bté): Used on French dolls to indicate that the patent is registered.

Character Doll: Dolls with heads modeled to look lifelike, such as infants, young or older children, young ladies, etc.

Crown Opening: The cut-away part of a doll head.

DEP: Abbreviation used on German and French dolls claiming registration.

D.R.G.M.: Abbreviation used on German dolls indicating a registered design or patent.

Embossed Mark: Raised letters, numbers, or names of the backs of heads or bodies.

Flange Neck: A doll's head with a ridge at the base of the neck which contains holes for sewing the head to a cloth body.

Flirting Eyes: Eyes which move from side to side as doll's head is tilted.

Frozen Charlotte: Doll molded all in one piece including arms and legs.

Ges. (Gesch.): Used on German dolls to indicate design is registered or patented.

Googly Eyes: Large often round eyes looking to the side; also called rougish or goo goo eyes.

Incised Mark: Letters, numbers or names impressed into the bisque on the back of the head or on the shoulder plate.

Intaglio Eyes: Painted eyes with sunken pupil and iris.

Kid Body: Body of white or pink leather.

Lustered China: China which has been given a pink tint to look more like real flesh color; also called pink-toned china.

Mohair: Goat's hair widely used in making doll wigs.

Molded Hair: Curls, waves, and comb marks which are actually part of the mold and not merely painted onto the head.

Open Mouth: Lips parted with an actual opening in the bisque, usually has teeth either molded in the bisque or set in separately and sometimes a tongue.

Open-closed Mouth: A mouth molded to appear open, but having no actual slit in the bisque.

Painted Bisque: Bisque covered with a layer of flesh-covered paint, which has not been baked in, so will easily rub or wash off.

Paperweight Eyes: Blown glass eyes which have depth and look real, usually found in French dolls.

Pate: A shaped piece of plaster, cork, cardboard, or other material which covers the crown opening.

Pierced Ears: Little holes through the doll's ear lobes to accommodate earrings.

Pierced-in Ears: A hole at the doll's earlobe which goes into the head to accommodate earrings.

Pink Bisque: A later bisque of about 1920 which was pre-colored pink.

Rembrandt Hair: Hair style parted in center with bangs at front, straight down sides and back and curled at ends.

S.G.D.G.: Used on French dolls to indicate that the patent is registered "without guarantee of the government"

Shoulder Head: A doll's head and shoulders all in one piece.

Shoulderplate: The actual shoulder portion sometimes molded in one with the head, sometimes a separate piece with a socket in which a head is inserted.

Socket Head: Head and neck which fit into an opening in the shoulderplate or the body.

Solid-dome Head: Head with no crown opening, could have painted hair or be covered by wig.

Stationary Eyes: Glass eyes which DO NOT move or sleep;also called fixed eyes.

Stone Bisque: Coarse white bisque of a lesser quality.

Toddler Body: Usually a chubby ball-jointed composition body with chunky, shorter thighs, and a diagonal hip joint;sometimes has curved instead of jointed arms;sometimes is of five pieces with straight chubby legs.

Turned Shoulder Head: Head and shoulders are one piece, but the head is molded at an angle so that the doll is not looking straight ahead.

Watermelon Mouth: Closed line-type mouth curved up at each side in an impish expression.

Wax Over: A doll of papier-mache or composition covered with a layer of wax to give a natural, lifelike finish.

Wire Eyes: Eyes which could be made to sleep by means of a wire which protruded from doll's head.

Selected Bibliography

Coleman, Dorothy, Elizabeth & Evelyn, THE COLLECTOR'S ENCYCLOPEDIA OF DOLLS, New York, New York

Angione, Genevieve, ALL-BISQUE AND HALF-BISQUE DOLLS, Nashville, Tennessee

Shoemaker, Rhoda, COMPO DOLLS CUTE & COLLECTIBLE, Volumes I & II, Menlo Park, California

Anderton, Johanna TWENTIETH CENTURY DOLLS, MORE TWENTIETH CENTURY DOLLS, Kansas City, Missouri

Merrill & Perkins, HANDBOOK OF COLLECTIBLE DOLLS, Volumes I, II, III, Saugus, Massachusetts

Selfridge & Cooper, DIMPLES & SAWDUST Volume I, Boulder, Colorado

Cooper, Marlowe, DIMPLES & SAWDUST Vol. II, Boulder, CO.

Selfridge, Madalaine, WENDY & FRIENDS, DOLLS IMAGES OF LOVE, Irving, California

Desmond, Kay, ALL COLOR BOOK OF DOLLS, New York, N.Y.

Noble, John, TREASURY OF BEAUTIFUL DOLLS, N.Y., N.Y.

Jacobsen, Carol, PORTRAIT OF DOLLS Volume I & II, Canonsburg, Pennsylvania

Smith, Pat, MODERN COLLECTORS DOLLS Volumes I & II, Paducah, Kentucky

Index